CCSS Prep
Grade 4
Editing and Revising

by Dana Konopka and Suzanne Borner

Edited by Patricia F. Braccio and Sarah M. Williams

Item Code: RAS 2709 • Copyright © 2013 Queue, Inc.

Queue, Inc. • 80 Hathaway Drive, Stratford, CT 06615
(800) 232-2224 • Fax: (800) 775-2729 • www.qworkbooks.com

TABLE OF CONTENTS

TO THE STUDENTS

In this editing and revising workbook, you will read many passages. You will then answer multiple-choice questions about what you have read.

As you read and answer the questions, please remember:

- You may refer back to the passage as often as you like.

- Read each question very carefully and choose the **best** answer.

- Indicate the correct multiple-choice answers directly in this workbook. Circle or underline the correct answer.

- Remember what you know about correct grammar, punctuation, and English usage.

Kelsey's fourth-grade class is learning about ocean life. Her teacher asked the students to imagine what they would see if they went down to the bottom of the ocean. She asked each student to describe life there. Kelsey took notes from her ocean book. Then she made an outline and wrote her rough draft. Now she needs your help editing and revising it.

Here is Kelsey's rough draft. Read it and then answer questions 1–11.

(1) How can anything live at the bottom of the ocean? (2) It's really dark and cold down there. (3) <u>They're</u> very little food. (4) I was surprised to learn that there are animals <u>that lives</u> on the bottom of the ocean! (5) Last summer, we stayed a week at a beach house near the ocean.

(6) There are fish called "dragonfish." (7) They have scales, and they have bodies like snakes. (8) <u>It swims</u> in water three thousand feet deep! (9) Giant sea spiders walk on the ocean floor they have super-long legs. (10) They are <u>more big</u> than the spiders we know. (11) The sea spiders can be two feet across. (12) The spiders are <u>carnivores they</u> suck the juice out of other <u>creters</u>.

(13) There are sea pens at the bottom of the ocean. (14) They are related by jellyfish. (15) They look weird. (16) They can live in water nineteen thousand feet deep. (17) Nineteen thousand feet is extremely deep.

1. Choose the correct way to write the underlined part of sentence 3.

   <u>They're</u> very little food.

   a. There's
   b. They is
   c. Their are
   d. No change is needed.

2. Choose the sentence that does **not** belong in the paragraph that begins with sentence 1.

   f. sentence 2
   g. sentence 1
   h. sentence 5
   j. sentence 4

1

3. Choose the correct way to write the underlined part of sentence 4.

   I was surprised to learn that there are animals <u>that lives</u> on the bottom of the ocean!

   a. that's live
   b. that living
   c. that live
   d. No change is needed.

4. Read sentence 9. It is poorly written.

   Giant sea spiders walk on the ocean floor they have super-long legs.

   Choose the **best** way to rewrite this sentence.

   f. Giant sea spiders walk on the ocean floor. They have super-long legs.
   g. Giant sea spiders walk on the ocean floor because they have super-long legs.
   h. Giant sea spiders walk on the ocean floor that they they have super-long legs.
   j. Giant sea spiders walk on the ocean floor, they have super-long legs.

5. Choose the correct way to write the underlined part of sentence 8.

   <u>It swims</u> in water three thousand feet deep!

   a. It swim
   b. They swim
   c. He swims
   d. No change is needed.

6. Read sentence 14. It is poorly written.

   They are related by jellyfish.

   Choose the **best** way to rewrite this sentence.

   f.   They are related to jellyfish.
   g.   They are related of jellyfish.
   h.   They are related with jellyfish.
   j.   They are related for jellyfish.

7. Choose the correct way to write the underlined part of sentence 10.

   They are <u>more big</u> than the spiders we know.

   a.   bigger
   b.   more bigger
   c.   biggest
   d.   No change is needed.

8. Kelsey wants to change sentence 15 so that it is more specific.

   They look <u>weird.</u>

   Choose the **best** way to rewrite the underlined part of the sentence.

   f.   like pointy things.
   g.   sharp.
   h.   like sharps things sticking out of the sand.
   j.   like sharp pens sticking out of the sand.

9. Choose the correct way to write this underlined part of sentence 12.

   The spiders are <u>carnivores they</u> suck the juice . . .

   a. carnivores, they,
   b. carnivores. They
   c. carnivores? They
   d. No change is needed.

10. Choose the **best** way to combine the ideas in sentences 16 and 17 into one sentence.

    They can live in water nineteen thousand feet deep. Nineteen thousand feet is extremely deep.

    f. They can live in extremely deep water of nineteen thousand feet.
    g. They can live in nineteen thousand feet extreme water.
    h. They can live in extremely deep nineteen thousand feet water.
    j. They can live in water nineteen thousand feet deep, which is extremely deep.

11. Choose the correct way to write this underlined part of sentence 12.

    . . . suck the juice out of other <u>creters</u>.

    a. creaters
    b. creatchers
    c. creatures
    d. No change is needed.

John is in the fourth grade. His class is planning to visit the science museum. John's teacher asked the students in the class to choose one astronaut and to write about him or her. John has written his rough draft, and now he needs your help editing and revising it.

Here is John's rough draft. Read it and then answer questions 1–11.

(1) Yuri Gagarin was the first person ever to travel in space. (2) He was born in <u>gzhatsk, a town in Russia.</u> (3) He studied to be an air force pilot, and then he <u>became a astronaut.</u> (4) I want to be an astronaut when I grow up.

(5) <u>Yuri's</u> space capsule was called the *Vostok*. (6) The name, *Vostok*, means "east" in Russian. (7) The *Vostok* had two parts. (8) One part was for Yuri. (9) The other part had oxygen and water <u>what he needed.</u> (10) Yuri orbited once around the whole planet on <u>april 12, 1961.</u> (11) He went more than seventeen thousand miles per hour! (12) The flight was one hour and forty-eight minutes long. (13) A computer controlled his return to earth.

(14) Unfortunately, Yuri <u>never makes</u> a second trip in space. (15) He died. (16) He is a Russian hero now. (17) Named after him was a crater on the moon.

1. Choose the correct way to write the underlined part of sentence 2.

   He was born in gzhatsk, a town in Russia.

   a. in gzhatsk, a town in russia.
   b. in gzhatsk, a Town in Russia.
   c. in Gzhatsk, a town in Russia.
   d. No change is needed.

2. Choose the topic sentence of this composition.

   f. I want to be an astronaut when I grow up.
   g. He is a Russian hero now.
   h. The flight was one hour and forty-eight minutes long.
   j. Yuri Gagarin was the first person ever to travel in space.

3. Choose the correct way to write the underlined part of sentence 3.

He studied to be an air force pilot, and then he <u>became a astronaut.</u>

a. became an astronaut.
b. became astronaut.
c. became some astronaut.
d. No change is needed.

4. Choose the sentence that is a supporting detail for sentence 10.

Yuri orbited once around the whole planet on <u>april 12, 1961.</u>

f. He is a Russian hero now.
g. He went more than seventeen thousand miles per hour!
h. The *Vostok* had two parts.
j. Yuri Gagarin was the first person ever to travel in space.

5. Choose the correct way to write the underlined part of sentence 5.

<u>Yuri's</u> space capsule was called the Vostok.

a. Yuris
b. Yuris'
c. Yuries'
d. No change is needed.

6. Choose the sentence that does **not** belong in the paragraph that begins with sentence 1.

f. sentence 2
g. sentence 1
h. sentence 4
j. sentence 3

7. Choose the correct way to write the underlined part of sentence 9.

    The other part had oxygen and water <u>what he needed.</u>

    a. that he needed.
    b. that needed.
    c. what needed him.
    d. No change is needed.

8. Read sentence 17. It is poorly written.

    Named after him was a crater on the moon.

    Choose the **best** way to rewrite this sentence.

    f. He named a crater on the moon.
    g. He named after a crater on the moon.
    h. A crater on the moon was named.
    j. A crater on the moon was named for him.

9. Choose the correct way to write the underlined part of sentence 10.

    Yuri orbited once around the whole planet on <u>april 12, 1961.</u>

    a. april 12 1961.
    b. april, 12, 1961.
    c. April 12, 1961.
    d. No change is needed.

10. John wants to change sentence 15 so that it is more specific.

   He died.

   Choose the **best** way to rewrite the sentence.

   f.   In 1968, he was killed in a plane crash.
   g.   He died in 1968.
   h.   He died in a plane.
   j.   He was killed in a plane crash.

11. Choose the correct way to write the underlined part of sentence 14.

   Unfortunately, Yuri <u>never makes</u> a second trip in space.

   a.   never make
   b.   never made
   c.   never making
   d.   No change is needed.

Josh is in the fourth grade. His class visited the Museum of Natural History. His teacher asked each student to write a thank-you letter to the director of the museum, telling what he or she liked best. Josh has written his rough draft, and now he needs your help editing and revising it.

Here is Josh's rough draft. Read it and then answer questions 1–10.

(1) Dear Mr. Donaghue

(2) I really enjoyed my trip to the Museum of Natural History <u>last monday.</u> (3) Thank you very much for letting us visit.

(4) I loved the dinosaur room the size of the big dinosaur was incredible. (5) I wonder how they put all those bones together. (6) I liked the dinosaur activity. (7) It was fun to put some dinosaur bones together. (8) I like to solve puzzles like that.

(9) The long painting on the wall in the dinosaur room was very impressive. (10) I could <u>look at him</u> for hours. (11) It helped me. (12) To see the history of the dinosaurs.

(13) The birds' part of the museum was beautiful and interesting. (14) Recognized were from my own backyard some birds that were there. (15) I also saw some that I had never seen before. (16) After, we went out for lunch.

(17) I also liked the dioramas. (18) <u>They were</u> very realistic. (19) They made me feel like I was standing right next to <u>the bears deer and sheep.</u>

(20) Thank you very much. (21) The Museum of Natural History is my favorite museum now.

(22) Sincerely,

(23) Josh Sussman

1. Choose the corrrect way to write line 1, the opening of the letter.

   Dear Mr. Donaghue

   a. Dear Mr. Donaghue,
   b. Dear Mr. Donaghue.
   c. Dear Mr. Donaghue!
   d. No change is needed.

2. Read sentence 4. It is poorly written.

   I loved the dinosaur room the size of the big dinosaur was incredible.

   Choose the **best** way to rewrite the sentence.

   f.   I loved the dinosaur room and the size of the big dinosaur was incredible.
   g.   I loved the dinosaur room, whose size of the big dinosaur was incredible.
   h.   I loved the dinosaur room. The size of the big dinosaur was incredible.
   j.   I loved the dinosaur room, the size of the big dinosaur was incredible.

3. Choose the correct way to write the underlined part of sentence 2.

   I really enjoyed my trip to the Museum of Natural History <u>last monday.</u>

   a.   last monday,
   b.   last Monday.
   c.   Last Monday.
   d.   No change is needed.

4. Read sentence 14. It is poorly written.

   Recognized were from my own backyard some birds that were there.

   Choose the **best** way to rewrite this sentence.

   f.   Recognized were some birds from my own backyard.
   g.   Some birds were recognized by my backyard.
   h.   I recognized some of my backyard there.
   j.   I recognized some birds there from my own backyard.

5. Choose the correct way to write the underlined part of sentence 10.

   I could <u>look at him</u> for hours.

   a. look at it
   b. look at them
   c. look at those
   d. No change is needed.

6. Choose the sentence that does **not** belong in the paragraph that begins with sentence 13.

   f. sentence 13
   g. sentence 14
   h. sentence 15
   j. sentence 16

7. Choose the correct way to write the underlined part of sentence 18.

   <u>They were</u> very realistic.

   a. They was
   b. Them were
   c. They is
   d. No change is needed.

8. Which one of these is **not** a complete sentence?

   f. It helped me.
   g. To see the history of the dinosaurs.
   h. Thank you very much.
   j. I also liked the dioramas.

9. Choose the correct way to write the underlined part of sentence 19.

   They made me feel like I was standing right next to <u>the bears deer and sheep.</u>

   a. the bears, deer, and, sheep.
   b. the bears. And deer and sheep.
   c. the bears, deer, and sheep.
   d. No change is needed.

10. Josh wants to add this sentence either to the paragraph that begins with sentence 17 or the paragraph that begins with sentence 20.

    I hope that I can come back someday soon.

    Where would the sentence **best** fit?

    f. right after sentence 17
    g. right after sentence 19
    h. right after sentence 20
    j. right after sentence 21

Jamal is in the fourth grade. His class is learning how to write autobiographies. An autobiography is a story of the author's own life. His teacher asked each student to write a short autobiography. Jamal brainstormed his thoughts, organized them, and wrote his rough draft. Now he needs your help editing and revising it.

Here is Jamal's rough draft. Read it and then answer questions 1—11.

(1) My name is Jamal Littleton, and I was born <u>on November 21, 1999.</u> (2) I was born in <u>alexandria, virginia</u>. (3) When I was five years old, my family moved. (4) To Huntington. (5) I started kindergarten that year. (6) My older brother had chicken pox when he was in kindergarten but I've never had them.

(7) I am a fourth grade student now. (8) I am in fourth grade at Smith Elementary School. (9) I have been there <u>for 2004</u>. (10) My <u>teachers</u> name is <u>Mr. Howard.</u> (11) He is a great teacher.

(12) I like school a lot and my favorite subjects are science and music and I also like to play soccer. (13) When I grow up, I want to be <u>a Scientist</u> and do research. (14) I want to find a better way to grow food. (15) I want there to be enough food for everybody in the world.

1. Choose the correct way to write the underlined part of sentence 1.

    My name is Jamal Littleton, and I was born <u>on November 21, 1999.</u>

    a. in November 21, 1999.
    b. on November 21 1999.
    c. on November, 21, 1999.
    d. No change is needed.

2. Choose the **best** way to combine the ideas in sentences 3 and 4 into one sentence.

When I was five years old, my family moved. To Huntington.

   f.   When I was five years old, my family moved.
   g.   When I was five years old, my family moved to Huntington.
   h.   To Huntington my family moved when I was five years old.
   j.   My family moved to Huntington, I was five years old.

3. Choose the correct way to write the underlined part of sentence 2.

I was born in <u>alexandria, virginia.</u>

   a.   Alexandria Virginia.
   b.   Alexandria, Virginia.
   c.   alexandria Virginia.
   d.   No change is needed.

4. Choose the sentence that does **not** belong in the paragraph that begins with sentence 1.

   f.   sentence 4
   g.   sentence 3
   h.   sentence 1
   j.   sentence 6

5. Choose the correct way to write the underlined part of sentence 10.

My <u>teachers</u> name is . . .

   a.   teachers'
   b.   teacher's
   c.   teaches
   d.   No change is needed.

14

6. Choose the **best** way to combine the ideas in sentences 7 and 8 into one sentence.

   I am a fourth grade student now. I am in fourth grade at Smith Elementary School.

   f. I am a fourth grade fourth grader at Smith Elementary School.
   g. I am a fourth grade student at Smith Elementary School.
   h. I am in the fourth grade as a student in Smith Elementary School.
   j. I am in Smith Elementary School and I am in fourth grade.

7. Choose the correct way to write the underlined part of sentence 9.

   I have been there <u>for 2004.</u>

   a. since four years.
   b. all 2004.
   c. since 2004.
   d. No change is needed.

8. Jamal wants to add this sentence to the paragraph that begins with sentence 7.

   He's smart and funny, but he's also tough and makes us work hard.

   Where would the sentence **best** fit?

   f. right after sentence 7
   g. right after sentence 8
   h. right after sentence 11
   j. right after sentence 9

9. Choose the correct way to write the underlined part of sentence 13.

   When I grow up, I want to be <u>a Scientist</u> and do research.

   a. a scientist
   b. an scientist
   c. A Scientist
   d. No change is needed.

10. Read sentence 12. It is poorly written.

   I like school a lot and my favorite subjects are science and music and I also like to play soccer.

   Choose the **best** way to rewrite the sentence.

   f. I like school a lot. I like science and music best. I like to play soccer too.
   g. I like school a lot. My favorite subjects are science and music. I also like to play soccer.
   h. I like school a lot and my favorite subjects are science and music. I also like to play soccer.
   j. I like school a lot. My favorite subjects are science and music and also, I like to play soccer.

11. Choose the correct way to write this underlined part of sentence 10.

   . . . name is <u>Mr. Howard.</u>

   a. mr. Howard.
   b. Mr Howard.
   c. Mr. howard.
   d. No change is needed.

16

Special's fourth-grade class recently visited the science museum. Her teacher asked each student to write a letter to a friend and to describe the visit. Special wrote her rough draft, but now she needs your help editing and revising it.

Here is Special's rough draft. Read it and then answer questions 1–10.

(1) Dear Erica,

(2) <u>On December 12 2008,</u> I went to a great place. (3) My class went to the science museum. (4) We had so much fun! (5) Because we got to do so many new and different hands-on activities.

(6) First, we saw the animals we got to watch them being fed. (7) Then, we went downstairs. (8) Used the weather station. (9) I could pretend I was a newscaster. (10) <u>I saw me</u> on TV! (11) After that, we went to a big room with all different kinds of robots. (12) We could go around the room and operate all of them. (13) My favorite thing was the planetarium show. (14) We learned about the stars in the night sky. (15) I had a cat named Star.

(16) I hope you can go to the science museum during <u>christmas vacation</u>. (17) <u>Yull</u> love it!

(18) Sincerely

(19) Special

1. Choose the correct way to write the underlined part of sentence 2.

   On December 12 2008, I went to a great place.

   a. On December, 12 2008
   b. On, December, 12, 2008,
   c. On December 12, 2008,
   d. No change is needed.

2. Read sentence 6. It is poorly written.

   First, we saw the animals we got to watch them being fed.

   Choose the **best** way to rewrite the sentence.

   f. First, we saw the animals and got to watch them being fed.
   g. First, we watched the animals that got fed.
   h. First, we saw the animals because we got to watch them being fed.
   j. First, we saw animals and then they got fed.

3. Choose the correct way to write the underlined part of sentence 10.

   <u>I saw me</u> on TV!

   a. I saw myself
   b. I see me
   c. I saw meself
   d. No change is needed.

4. Choose the sentence that does **not** belong in the paragraph that begins with sentence 6.

   f. My favorite thing was the planetarium show.
   g. I had a cat named Star.
   h. Dear Erica,
   j. I could pretend I was a newscaster.

5. Choose the correct way to write the underlined part of sentence 17.

   <u>Yull</u> love it!

   a. Youll
   b. You'll
   c. youl'l
   d. No change is needed.

6. Choose the **best** way to combine the ideas in sentences 4 and 5 into one sentence.

   We had so much fun! Because we got to do so many new and different hands-on activities.

   f. Hands-on activities are new, different, and so much fun!
   g. Because of that we got to do so many new and different hands-on activities, we had so much fun!
   h. We had so much fun, because we got to do so many new and different hands-on activities.
   j. We had so much fun because we got to do so many new and different hands-on activities!

7. Choose the correct way to write the underlined part of sentence 16.

   I hope you can go to the science museum during <u>christmas vacation.</u>

   a. christmas Vacation.
   b. christmas, vacation.
   c. Christmas vacation.
   d. No change is needed.

8. Special wants to add this sentence to the paragraph that begins with sentence 6.

   I never knew there were so many constellations.

   Where would the sentence **best** fit?

   f. right after sentence 6
   g. right after sentence 12
   h. right after sentence 14
   j. right after sentence 15

9. Choose the correct way to write line 18, the closing of the letter.

    Sincerely

    a. Sincerely,
    b. sincerely,
    c. Sincerely.
    d. No change is needed.

10. Which one of these is **not** a complete sentence?

    f. Then, we went downstairs.
    g. Used the weather station.
    h. I could pretend I was a newscaster.
    j. We had so much fun!

Erin is in the fourth grade. Her class is studying money. Her teacher asked each student to research the history of money and then to write a short report. Erin went to the library and took notes. She organized them and wrote her rough draft. Now she needs your help editing and revising it.

Here is Erin's rough draft. Read it and then answer questions 1–11.

(1) A long time ago, <u>their</u> was no such thing as money. (2) If you wanted something, you had to barter that means you had to trade.

(3) Then came simple money. (4) The first money <u>didn't look</u> like our money today. (5) Money then could be anything that people used to buy something. (6) The first money was made of <u>beans shells or beads.</u> (7) Some people used animal hides. (8) Animals too.

(9) The first metal coins were made about two thousand and five hundred years ago in Turkey. (10) My grandfather has a cool coin collection. (11) People liked to use metal because <u>they was strong.</u> (12) It also lasted a long time.

(13) Paper money was invented <u>in china.</u> (14) Chinese people started buying things with pieces of paper. (15) They started this about two thousand and five hundred years ago. (16) People in other countries didn't like that idea. (17) That's <u>becus</u> they thought that paper was not worth anything. (18) It took a long time for the rest of the world to start using paper money.

1. Choose the correct way to write the underlined part of sentence 1.

   A long time ago, <u>their</u> was no such thing as money.

   a. they're
   b. there
   c. the
   d. No change is needed.

2. Choose the sentence that does **not** belong in the paragraph that begins with sentence 9.

    f.   sentence 12
    g. sentence 11
    h. sentence 10
    j.   sentence 9

3. Choose the correct way to write the underlined part of sentence 4.

The first money <u>didn't look</u> like our money today.

    a. didnt look
    b. did't look
    c. did'nt look
    d. No change is needed.

4. Read sentence 2. It is poorly written.

If you wanted something, you had to barter that means you had to trade.

Choose the **best** way to rewrite the sentence.

    f.   If you wanted something, you had to barter that which means you had to trade.
    g. If you wanted something, you had to barter means you had to trade.
    h. If you wanted something, you had to barter. That means you had to trade.
    j.   If you wanted something, you had to barter and trade.

22

5. Choose the correct way to write the underlined part of sentence 6.

    The first money was made of <u>beans shells or beads.</u>

    a. beans or shells or beads.
    b. beans, shells or, beads.
    c. beans, shells, or beads.
    d. No change is needed.

6. Choose the **best** way to combine the ideas in sentences 14 and 15 into one sentence.

    Chinese people started buying things with pieces of paper. They started this about two thousand and five hundred years ago.

    f. Chinese people started buying things with pieces of paper, about two thousand and five hundred years ago.
    g. Chinese people started buying paper about two thousand and five hundred years ago.
    h. Chinese people started buying two thousand and five hundred years ago.
    j. Chinese people started buying things with pieces of paper about two thousand and five hundred years ago.

7. Choose the correct way to write the underlined part of sentence 11.

    People liked to use metal because <u>they was strong.</u>

    a. it was strong.
    b. he was strong.
    c. they were strong.
    d. No change is needed.

8. Which one of these is **not** a complete sentence?

    f. Then came simple money.
    g. Some people used animal hides.
    h. They started this about two thousand and five hundred years ago.
    j. Animals too.

9. Choose the correct way to write the underlined part of sentence 13.

    Paper money was invented <u>in china.</u>

    a. in China.
    b. In china.
    c. In China.
    d. No change is needed.

10. Choose the sentence that **best** fits right after sentence 18.

    f. Anything could have been used as money.
    g. Now, however, paper money is commonly used worldwide.
    h. Can you imagine trading your pet dog for a can of oil?
    j. Coins, of course, are still used today.

11. Choose the correct way to write the underlined part of sentence 17.

    That's <u>becus</u> they thought that paper was not worth anything.

    a. becauze
    b. becuz
    c. because
    d. No change is needed.

Luke is in the fourth grade. His class is learning about endangered species. His teacher asked each student to choose one endangered species, to explain why it is endangered, and to tell what is being done about it. Luke chose to write about the giant panda. Luke wrote his rough draft, and now he needs your help editing and revising it.

Here is Luke's rough draft. Read it and then answer questions 1–10.

(1) Giant pandas are members of the bear family. (2) They are shaped like bears, and <u>it's</u> black and white. (3) Their Chinese name means "black and white cat-footed animal." (4) They live in the mountains in China. (5) <u>It rained</u> a lot where they live. (6) I enjoy the rain because I find it to be very soothing.

(7) The giant panda is an endangered species. (8) <u>There is</u> only about one thousand pandas. (9) They are endangered because their food is running out. (10) A panda needs up to forty <u>Pounds of bamboo</u> per day! (11) Humans are moving into <u>the pandas areas.</u> (12) Farming and logging are taking away the bamboo. (13) Hunting is another reason that the panda is endangered. (14) To hunt pandas is illegal against the law. (15) However, some people still try to kill them for their fur. (16) They kill the pandas so that they can get the fur.

(17) The Chinese are trying to save the giant pandas. (18) They are trying to make better bamboo. (19) This bamboo would be stronger and would grow back better. (20) I hope this works. (21) It would be a shame to lose the giant pandas!

1. Choose the correct way to write the underlined part of sentence 2.

   They are shaped like bears, and <u>it's</u> black and white.

   a. they're
   b. he's
   c. is
   d. No change is needed.

2. Choose the sentence that does **not** belong in the paragraph that begins with sentence 1.

    f.   sentence 3
    g.   sentence 1
    h.   sentence 6
    j.   sentence 4

3. Choose the correct way to write the underlined part of sentence 5.

   It rained a lot where they live.

    a.   They rained
    b.   It's raining
    c.   It rains
    d.   No change is needed.

4. Choose the topic sentence for the paragraph that begins with sentence 7.

    f.   Hunting is another reason that the panda is endangered.
    g.   The giant panda is an endangered species.
    h.   To hunt pandas is illegal against the law.
    j.   Farming and logging are taking away the bamboo.

5. Choose the correct way to write the underlined part of sentence 8.

   There is only about one thousand pandas.

    a.   There being
    b.   There are
    c.   It is
    d.   No change is needed.

6. Luke wants to add this sentence to the paragraph that begins with sentence 7.

    The main thing a panda eats is bamboo.

    Where would the sentence **best** fit?

    f. right after sentence 9
    g. right after sentence 10
    h. right after sentence 16
    j. right after sentence 8

7. Choose the correct way to write the underlined part of sentence 10.

    A panda needs up to forty <u>Pounds of bamboo</u> per day!

    a. Pounds of Bamboo
    b. pounds of bamboo
    c. Pounds bamboo
    d. No change is needed.

8. Read sentence 14. It is poorly written.

    To hunt pandas is illegal against the law.

    Choose the **best** way to rewrite this sentence.

    f. To hunt is against the law.
    g. Against the law is panda hunting.
    h. To hunt pandas is against the illegal law.
    j. To hunt pandas is against the law.

27

9. Choose the correct way to write the underlined part of sentence 11.

   Humans are moving into <u>the pandas areas.</u>

   a. the pandas' areas.
   b. the pandas's areas.
   c. the panda's areas.
   d. No change is needed.

10. Choose the **best** way to combine the ideas in sentences 15 and 16 into one sentence.

   However, some people still try to kill them for their fur. They kill the pandas so that they can get the fur.

   f. However, some people still try to kill them the pandas so that they can get the fur.
   g. However, some people still try it.
   h. However, some people still try to kill pandas for their fur.
   j. However, some people still try to kill.

Mary is in the fourth grade. Her class is studying American history. Her teacher asked each student to write a letter to a famous person from history. Mary chose to write to Harriet Beecher Stowe. She organized her ideas and wrote her rough draft. Now, she needs your help editing and revising it.

Here is Mary's rough draft. Read it and then answer questions 1–11.

(1) Dear Mrs. Stowe

(2) I visited your house in <u>Hartford Connecticut</u> last year. (3) It is beautiful I learned a lot about you there. (4) Afterwards, we all went out for hamburgers.

(5) <u>I'm</u> really glad that you wrote *Uncle Tom's Cabin*. (6) It made people think about slavery. (7) I guess it caused a lot of trouble, though. (8) It made angry many people. (9) Abraham Lincoln called you "the little lady who made this big war." (10) He was talking about the Civil War! (11) Do you really think it is <u>posibel</u> that you started the Civil War?

(12) You had such a big family! (13) Did your children ever help you write? (14) I heard you supported your family by writing. (15) You didn't just write *Uncle Tom's Cabin*. (16) Poems, too. (17) You wrote <u>religious books children's books and novels for grown-ups.</u> (18) I'm glad that you wrote so many things. (19) We will always remember <u>yore</u> ideas.

(20) Sincerely,

(21) Mary Soltis

1. Choose the correct way to write line 1, the opening of the letter.

   Dear Mrs. Stowe

   a. Dear Mrs. Stowe,
   b. Dear mrs. Stowe
   c. Dear Misses Stowe
   d. No change is needed.

2. Read sentence 3. It is poorly written.

   It is beautiful I learned a lot about you there.

   Choose the **best** way to rewrite the sentence.

   f.   It is beautiful because I learned a lot about you there.
   g.   It is beautiful. I learned a lot about you there.
   h.   It is beautiful so I learned a lot about you there.
   j.   It is beautiful, I learned a lot about you there.

3. Choose the correct way to write the underlined part of sentence 2.

   I visited your house in <u>Hartford Connecticut</u> last year.

   a.   hartford, Connecticut
   b.   Hartford Connecticut
   c.   Hartford, Connecticut,
   d.   No change is needed.

4. Choose the sentence that does **not** belong either in the paragraph that begins with sentence 2 or the paragraph that begins with sentence 5.

   f.   sentence 9
   g.   sentence 11
   h.   sentence 3
   j.   sentence 4

5. Choose the correct way to write the underlined part of sentence 5.

   <u>I'm really glad that you wrote</u> Uncle Tom's Cabin.

   a.   i'm
   b.   Im
   c.   Im'
   d.   No change is needed.

6. Read sentence 8. It is poorly written.

   It made angry many people.

   Choose the **best** way to rewrite this sentence.

   f. It made many people angry.
   g. It made me angry.
   h. Many people were angry.
   j. People are angry.

7. Choose the correct way to write the underlined part of sentence 11.

   Do you really think it is <u>posibel</u> that you started the Civil War?

   a. posible
   b. possibel
   c. possible
   d. No change is needed.

8. Which one of these is **not** a complete sentence?

   f. It made people think about slavery.
   g. I guess it caused a lot of trouble, though.
   h. You didn't just write *Uncle Tom's Cabin*.
   j. Poems, too.

9. Choose the correct way to write the underlined part of sentence 17.

   You wrote <u>religious books children's books and novels for grown-ups.</u>

   a. religious books. Children's books and novels for grown-ups.
   b. religious books, children's books, and novels for grown-ups.
   c. religious books and children's books and novels for grown-ups.
   d. No change is needed.

10. Mary wants to add this sentence to the paragraph that begins with sentence 12.

    I hope to have read them all by the time I graduate from high school.

    Where would the sentence **best** fit?

    f. right after sentence 15
    g. right after sentence 16
    h. right after sentence 18
    j. right after sentence 19

11. Choose the correct way to write the underlined part of sentence 19.

    We will always remember <u>yore</u> ideas.

    a. you're
    b. your
    c. your'e
    d. No change is needed.

32

Isaac is in the fourth grade. His art class is studying crafts. His teacher asked each student in the class to choose one type of craft and to explain how it is made. Isaac chose to write about hand-made glass. He took notes from his library book, organized them, and wrote his rough draft. Now he needs your help editing and revising it.

Here is part of Isaac's rough draft. Read it and then answer questions 1–9.

(1) The very first glass bottles were made the "sand-core" way. (2) There <u>were</u> a lump of sand or clay on the end of a rod. (3) The rod <u>was dipped into melted glass</u>

(4) A new way of making glass was invented in the first century B.C.E. (5) The rod was made hollow. (6) The glassmaker could blow down the center of the rod. (7) Glassblowing was invented. (8) This was the beginning of glassblowing as we know it today.

(9) This is how glassblowing works the melted glass sits in a big pot. (10) The rod picks up some of the glass, and the blower blows a little bubble into it. (11) The blower <u>turned</u> the rod over and over. (12) Sometimes the glass gets rolled on <u>an iron slab.</u> (13) This helps to get the right shape. (14) If the glass gets too hard. (15) It goes into the furnace again. (16) The glassblower can make a lot of different shapes. (17) He can make a bottle, a jug, <u>a bole,</u> a jar, or a vase. (18) My mom has a lot of different vases at home.

1. Choose the correct way to write the underlined part of sentence 2.

    There <u>were</u> a lump of sand or clay on the end of a rod.

    a. are
    b. where
    c. was
    d. No change is needed.

2. Choose the sentence that does **not** belong in the paragraph that begins with sentence 9.

    f. sentence 18
    g. sentence 13
    h. sentence 15
    j. sentence 11

3. Choose the correct way to write the underlined part of sentence 3.

    The rod <u>was dipped into melted glass</u>

    a. was dipped into melted glass.
    b. was dipped into melted glass,
    c. was dipped into melted glass?
    d. No change is needed.

4. Choose the **best** way to combine the ideas in sentences 7 and 8 into one sentence.

    Glassblowing was invented. This was the beginning of glassblowing as we know it today.

    f. This glassblowing works.
    g. We know that glassblowing was invented today.
    h. Glassblowing was invented today, as we know it.
    j. Glassblowing, as we know it today, was invented.

5. Choose the correct way to write the underlined part of sentence 11.

    The blower <u>turned</u> the rod over and over.

    a. turning
    b. was turning
    c. turns
    d. No change is needed.

6. Which one of these is **not** a complete sentence?

    f. This helps to get the right shape.
    g. The rod was made hollow.
    h. This helps to get the right shape.
    j. If the glass gets too hard.

7. Choose the correct way to write the underlined part of sentence 12.

   Sometimes the glass gets rolled on <u>an iron slab.</u>

   a. any iron slab.
   b. an slab of iron.
   c. an iron, slab.
   d. No change is needed.

8. Read sentence 9. It is poorly written.

   This is how glassblowing works the melted glass sits in a big pot.

   Choose the **best** way to rewrite the sentence.

   f. This is how glassblowing works, the melted glass sits in a big pot.
   g. This is how glassblowing works. The melted glass sits in a big pot.
   h. This is how glassblowing works? The melted glass sits in a big pot.
   j. This is how glassblowing works! the melted glass sits in a big pot.

9. Choose the correct way to write the underlined part of sentence 17.

   He can make a bottle, a jug, <u>a bole,</u> a jar, or a vase.

   a. a bowl,
   b. a boll,
   c. a bowel,
   d. No change is needed.

Maria is in the fourth grade. Her class is studying earthquakes. Maria wanted to know what makes earthquakes happen. She took a book out of the library, took notes, and wrote the rough draft of a short report. Now she needs your help editing and revising it.

Here is Maria's rough draft. Read it and then answer questions 1–10.

---

(1) What causes earthquakes? (2) The earth is covered with a layer of rock. (3) It is like a thin shell that covers the hot liquid inside the earth. (4) This layer is not just one big piece of rock. (5) <u>They have</u> different pieces that are called "plates." (6) The plates are always moving they move so slowly that we can't feel it. (7) Sometimes pressure builds up for a long time. (8) All of sudden, move! (9) That movement is an earthquake.

(10) <u>There are</u> three kinds of earthquakes. (11) They usually happen along the lines between the plates. (12) Sometimes the plates are moving apart. (13) This is called an "extension earthquake." (14) These are <u>the less severe kind</u> of earthquake. (15) Sometimes the plates slide past each other. (16) That is called a "transform," and it usually causes medium earthquakes. (17) The San Andreas Fault in <u>california</u> is a transform. (18) The worst kind of earthquake is a "compression earthquake." (19) This is when plates hit. (20) Alaska and Chile have compression lines.

(21) We don't have any big fault lines where we live. (22) No wonder we have never had a bad earthquake here. (23) i'm glad!

---

1. Choose the correct way to write the underlined part of sentence 5.

   <u>They have</u> different pieces that are called "plates."

   a. It has
   b. These have
   c. Those have
   d. No change is needed.

36

2. Read sentence 8. It is poorly written.

   All of sudden, move!

   Choose the **best** way to rewrite this sentence.

   f. All of a sudden, they move!
   g. All of sudden, they move!
   h. Suddenly, there move!
   j. Suddenly, move!

3. Choose the correct way to write the underlined part of sentence 10.

   <u>There are</u> three kinds of earthquakes.

   a. There is
   b. There was
   c. There being
   d. No change is needed.

4. Choose the sentence that is a supporting detail for the information about the various kinds of earthquakes.

   f. The earth is covered with a layer of rock.
   g. The plates are always moving they move so slowly that we can't feel it.
   h. Sometimes the plates slide past each other.
   j. We don't have any big fault lines where we live.

5. Choose the correct way to write the underlined part of sentence 14.

   These are <u>the less severe kind</u> of earthquake.

   a. the lesser severe kind
   b. the least severe kind
   c. the most less severe kind
   d. No change is needed.

37

6. Read sentence 6. It is poorly written.

   The plates are always moving they move so slowly that we can't feel it.

   Choose the **best** way to rewrite the sentence.

   f. The plates are always moving because they move so slowly that we can't feel it.
   g. The plates are always moving? They move so slowly that we can't feel it.
   h. The plates are always moving that we can't feel it.
   j. The plates are always moving. They move so slowly that we can't feel it.

7. Choose the correct way to write the underlined part of sentence 17.

   The San Andreas Fault in <u>california</u> is a transform.

   a. the California
   b. california,
   c. California
   d. No change is needed.

8. Maria wants to change sentence 19 so that it is more specific.

   This is when <u>plates hit.</u>

   Choose the **best** way to rewrite the underlined part of the sentence.

   f. the plates press together and cause violent movement on the ground.
   g. plates are violent.
   h. plates are moving in the ground.
   j. the plates press together cause violence on the ground.

9. Choose the correct way to write sentence 23.

   i'm glad!

   a. I'm glad!
   b. im glad!
   c. im' glad!
   d. No change is needed.

10. Maria wants to add this sentence to the paragraph that begins with sentence 1.

    The earth rumbles and shakes.

    Where would the sentence **best** fit?

    f. right after sentence 1
    g. right after sentence 8
    h. right after sentence 9
    j. right after sentence 2

Kevin's fourth-grade class is learning about American history. His teacher asked each student to write about an interesting person in the history of our country. Kevin chose to write about Tom Thumb. He has written his rough draft, and now he needs your help editing and revising it.

Here is Kevin's rough draft. Read it and then answer questions 1–10.

(1) "Tom Thumb" was born in <u>bridgeport, Connecticut,</u> in 1838. (2) His real name was Charles Sherwood Stratton. (3) He was the son of carpenter. (4) His parents were average-sized, but Charles was a "dwarf." (5) A dwarf is a person who is very, very short. (6) I am the shortest person in my class.

(7) There was a man in town named P.T. Barnum. (8) He was in show business. (9) He discovered Charles in 1842. (10) When Charles was four years old. (11) He was only twenty-five inches tall. (12) P.T. Barnum gave Charles the name, Tom Thumb. (13) He took Tom Thumb around <u>the World</u> so that people could see him. (14) <u>Tom Thumb learns</u> how to sing, dance, and act. (15) He visited <u>president lincoln</u> and the Queen of England. (16) He visited some really famous people.

(17) Tom Thumb got married. (18) They got married in <u>new york city,</u> and there were two thousand people at their wedding. (19) When Tom Thumb died in 1883, ten thousand people came to his funeral. (20) He was one of America's <u>favrit</u> people.

1. Choose the correct way to write the underlined part of sentence 1.

"Tom Thumb" was born in <u>bridgeport, Connecticut,</u> in 1838.

a. bridgeport, connecticut,
b. Bridgeport, Connecticut,
c. Bridgeport, connecticut,
d. No change is needed.

2. Read sentence 3. It is poorly written.

   He was the son of carpenter.

   Choose the **best** way to rewrite this sentence.

   f. He was son of carpenter.
   g. He was the son of a carpenter.
   h. His son was a carpenter.
   j. He was a son and a carpenter.

3. Choose the correct way to write the underlined part of sentence 13.

   He took Tom Thumb around <u>the World</u> so that people could see him.

   a. the world
   b. The World
   c. the, World
   d. No change is needed.

4. Choose the sentence that does **not** belong in the paragraph that begins with sentence 1.

   f. sentence 1
   g. sentence 2
   h. sentence 4
   j. sentence 6

5. Choose the correct way to write the underlined part of sentence 14.

   <u>Tom Thumb learns</u> how to sing, dance, and act.

   a. Tom Thumb learning
   b. Tom Thumb will learn
   c. Tom Thumb learned
   d. No change is needed.

41

6. Choose the **best** way to combine the ideas in sentences 10 and 11 into one sentence.

When Charles was four years old. He was only twenty-five inches tall.

    f.   When Charles was only twenty-five inches tall, he was four years old.
    g.   When Charles was four years old, he was only twenty-five inches tall.
    h.   Charles was only twenty-five at four.
    j.   At four, Charles was only twenty-five.

7. Choose the correct way to write the underlined part of sentence 15.

He visited <u>president lincoln</u> and the Queen of England.

    a.   president Lincoln
    b.   President lincoln
    c.   President Lincoln
    d.   No change is needed.

8. Kevin wants to change sentence 17 so that it is more specific.

Tom Thumb got married.

Choose the **best** way to rewrite the sentence.

    f.   Tom Thumb married a woman in 1863.
    g.   Lavinia and Tom got married in 1863.
    h.   Tom Thumb got married in 1863.
    j.   In 1863, Tom Thumb married Lavinia Warren.

9. Choose the correct way to write the underlined part of sentence 18.

   They got married in <u>new york city,</u> and there were two thousand people at their wedding.

   a. New york city,
   b. New York City,
   c. new York city,
   d. No change is needed.

10. Choose the correct way to write the underlined part of sentence 20.

   He was one of America's <u>favrit</u> people.

   f. favorite
   g. faveritt
   h. faverite
   j. No change is needed.

Justin's fourth-grade class is planning to visit the symphony. His music class is learning about the instruments of the orchestra. His teacher asked each student to pretend to be one instrument and to describe the orchestra from that instrument's point of view. Justin chose the cymbals. He wrote his rough draft, and now he needs your help editing and revising it.

Here is Justin's rough draft. Read it and then answer questions 1–10.

(1) I am a cymbal. (2) I am a percussion instrument. (3) <u>Drums gongs triangles</u> are also percussion instruments. (4) <u>The zildjian</u> Company in the United States made me by a secret method. (5) I feel very special! (6) I don't mean to <u>boste</u>, but I am a shiny gold color. (7) I am shaped like a broad-brimmed hat. (8) I have a leather handle in the middle. (9) Sometimes I am hung on a stand and hit with a mallet. (10) Usually, into the other cymbal I just crash.

(11) The only thing I don't like is having to wait. (12) Sometimes <u>a song had</u> no cymbals until the very end. (13) Then it's boring to sit <u>thru</u> the whole song. (14) I'm glad that I can sit next to my friends. (15) The drums.

(16) I like where I sit in the orchestra. (17) I get to see everything. (18) There are a lot of musicians there. (19) <u>There is</u> only one pair of cymbals! (20) I love to hang out with my friends after the show.

1. Choose the correct way to write the underlined part of sentence 3.

   <u>Drums gongs triangles</u> are also percussion instruments.

   a. Drums, and gongs, and triangles
   b. Drums gongs, triangles
   c. Drums, gongs, and triangles
   d. No change is needed.

44

2. Read sentence 10. It is poorly written.

   Usually, into the other cymbal I just crash.

   Choose the **best** way to rewrite this sentence.

   f. Usually, I just crash into the other cymbals.
   g. The other cymbal and I had a crash.
   h. `Usually, I just crashed into the other cymbal.
   j. Usually, I just crash into the other cymbal.

3. Choose the correct way to write the underlined part of sentence 4.

   The zildjian Company in the United States made me by a secret method.

   a. The Zildjian
   b. the zildjian
   c. The zildjian,
   d. No change is needed.

4. Choose the sentence that **best** fits right after sentence 16.

   f. I don't know where I like to sit.
   g. Although I know I'm just a cymbal, I have feelings.
   h. I have been waiting all night.
   j. I am happy to sit in the back behind all of the violins.

5. Choose the correct way to write the underlined part of sentence 6.

   I don't mean to boste, but I am a shiny gold color.

   a. boost
   b. boast
   c. bosed
   d. No change is needed.

6. Which one of these is **not** a complete sentence?

    f.   The drums.
    g. I'm glad that I can sit next to my friends.
    h. I like where I sit in the orchestra.
    j. I get to see everything.

7. Choose the correct way to write the underlined part of sentence 12.

    Sometimes <u>a song had</u> no cymbals until the very end.

    a. a song has
    b. a song having
    c. a song have
    d. No change is needed.

8. Choose the correct way to write the underlined part of sentence 13.

    Then it's boring to sit <u>thru</u> the whole song.

    f.   though
    g. threw
    h. through
    j. No change is needed.

9. Justin wants to change sentence 18 so that it is more specific.

   There are <u>a lot of musicians there.</u>

   Choose the **best** way to rewrite the underlined part of the sentence.

   a. more than seventy musicians in the whole orchestra.
   b. so many musicians in the whole orchestra.
   c. seventy-two musicians in the whole orchestra.
   d. tons of musicians in the whole orchestra.

10. Choose the correct way to write the underlined part of sentence 19.

    <u>There is</u> only one pair of cymbals!

    f. There are
    g. They're
    h. There were
    j. No change is needed.

Jose's fourth-grade class heard *The Turtle Story*, a story told by the Gabrielino Native Americans of California. This story explains what causes earthquakes. His teacher asked each student to summarize the story in his or her own words. Jose wrote a rough draft and now he needs your help to edit and revise it.

Here is Jose's rough draft. Read it and then answer questions 1–10.

(1) When the earth first began, there <u>were</u> nothing but water. (2) The Great Spirit looked down and decided to make some land. (3) He looked and looked until he found a turtle with a huge back. (4) The back made a nice island. (5) He asked the turtle to go get six of his brothers. (6) After six days, he returned with his brothers and then there were seven turtles.

(7) The Great Spirit lined up the turtles. (8) <u>He told him</u> not to move. (9) He put dirt and straw on <u>them backs.</u> (10) He made them as continents.

(11) The turtles were not happy where they were four of them wanted to go east three of them wanted to go west. (12) <u>They decide</u> to split up. (13) The earth started shaking. (14) The turtles could not get very far because they were so heavy. (15) They had to stay put and stop arguing.

(16) The turtles can never <u>stay happy long time.</u> (17) Then they fight again and try to move a little more. (18) Every time they start arguing and moving again, another California earthquake starts. (19) I've never experienced an earthquake in real life.

1. Choose the correct way to write the underlined part of sentence 1.

    When the earth first began, there <u>were</u> nothing but water.

    a. was
    b. wasn't
    c. weren't
    d. No change is needed.

2. Read sentence 10. It is poorly written.

    He made them as continents.

    Choose the **best** way to rewrite this sentence.

    f. He made continents.
    g. He made them into continents.
    h. He put them on continents.
    j. He put continents out on them.

3. Choose the correct way to write the underlined part of sentence 8.

    <u>He told him</u> not to move.

    a. He told it
    b. He told her
    c. He told them
    d. No change is needed.

4. Choose the topic sentence for the paragraph that begins with sentence 1.

    f. When the earth first began, there were nothing but water.
    g. The back made a nice island.
    h. It took six days, and then there were seven turtles.
    j. The Great Spirit looked down and decided to make some land.

5. Choose the correct way to write the underlined part of sentence 9.

    He put dirt and straw on <u>them backs.</u>

    a. his backs.
    b. their backs.
    c. its back.
    d. No change is needed.

6. Choose the sentence that does **not** belong in the paragraph that begins with sentence 16.

    f.   sentence 19
    g.   sentence 17
    h.   sentence 18
    j.   sentence 16

7. Choose the correct way to write the underlined part of sentence 12.

    They decide to split up.

    a.   They will decide
    b.   They decided
    c.   The decision
    d.   No change is needed.

8. Choose the correct way to write the underlined part of sentence 16.

    The turtles can never stay happy long time.

    f.   stay happy since a long time.
    g.   stay happy since many years.
    h.   stay happy for a long time.
    j.   No change is needed.

9. Read sentence 11. It is poorly written.

   The turtles were not happy where they were four of them wanted to go east three of them wanted to go west.

   Choose the **best** way to rewrite the sentence.

   a. The turtles were not happy where they were and four of them wanted to go east and three of them wanted to go west.
   b. The turtles were not happy where they were because four of them wanted to go east because three of them wanted to go west.
   c. The turtles were not happy where they were, four of them wanted to go east, three of them wanted to go west.
   d. The turtles were not happy where they were. Four of them wanted to go east. Three of them wanted to go west.

10. Jose wants to add this sentence to the paragraph that begins with sentence 1.

    The turtle did exactly what the Great Spirit had asked.

    Where would this sentence **best** fit?

    f. right after sentence 6
    g. right after sentence 1
    h. right after sentence 5
    j. right after sentence 3

Emma is in the fourth grade. Her teacher asked each student to compare and contrast two different types of maps. Emma took notes from her textbook and her library book. Then she wrote her rough draft. Now she needs your help editing and revising it.

Here is Emma's rough draft. Read it and then answer questions 1–11.

(1) A navigation map and a topographic <u>map is</u> very different. (2) Most people use navigation maps. (3) Those are the kind you buy at the store that are so hard to fold back up. (4) They show you where all of the streets and highways are. (5) They help you to know. (6) Which way to go.

(7) A topographic map shows the shape of the earth's <u>surface it</u> does this with contour lines. (8) These are lines that show which places are the same height. (9) You can tell a lot of things with a topographic map. (10) <u>it's lines</u> show you the height of mountains. (11) You can see how deep is the ocean. (12) You can tell how steep mountain slopes are.

(13) Navigation maps and topographic maps have some things in common. (14) Each kind of map <u>can show</u> both streams and buildings. (15) Sometimes topographic maps show roads, too. (16) There are topographical maps of <u>north america</u> in my hiking book. (17) They show us where to find the hills for hiking.

(18) I think navigation maps are <u>usefuller than</u> topographical maps. (19) People drive more than they hike. (20) One time my family and I drove to California and back.

1. Choose the correct way to write the underlined part of sentence 1.

   A navigation map and a topographic <u>map is</u> very different.

   a. maps is
   b. map, is
   c. map are
   d. No change is needed.

2. Choose the sentence that is **not** a supporting detail from the paragraph that begins with sentence 7.

    f. These are lines that show which places are the same height.
    g. You can tell a lot of things with a topographic map.
    h. You can tell how steep mountain slopes are.
    j. You can see how deep is the ocean.

3. Choose the correct way to write the underlined part of sentence 7.

A topographic map shows the shape of the earth's <u>surface it</u> does this with contour lines.

    a. surface. It
    b. surface, it
    c. surface? It
    d. No change is needed.

4. Read sentence 11. It is poorly written.

You can see how deep is the ocean.

Choose the **best** way to rewrite this sentence.

    f. You can see that the ocean is deep.
    g. You can see how deep the ocean is.
    h. You can see the deep ocean.
    j. You can see the ocean.

5. Choose the correct way to write the underlined part of sentence 10.

<u>it's lines</u> show you the height of mountains.

    a. It's lines
    b. It lines
    c. Its lines
    d. No change is needed.

6. Choose the sentence that does **not** belong either in the paragraph that begins with sentence 13 or the paragraph that begins with sentence 18.

    f.   sentence 13
    g.   sentence 20
    h.   sentence 16
    j.   sentence 17

7. Choose the correct way to write the underlined part of sentence 14.

    Each kind of map <u>can show</u> both streams and buildings.

    a. showing
    b. did show
    c. showed
    d. No change is needed.

8. Choose the **best** way to combine the ideas in sentences 5 and 6 into one sentence.

    They help you to know. Which way to go.

    f.   They help you to go to where you know.
    g.   They help you know and go.
    h.   They help you to know which way to go.
    j.   They know which way to help you go.

9. Choose the correct way to write the underlined part of sentence 16.

    There are topographical maps of <u>north america</u> in my hiking book.

    a. North America
    b. North america
    c. Northern America
    d. No change is needed.

10. Emma wants to add this sentence to the paragraph that begins with sentence 7.

   This is especially helpful for hikers.

   Where would the sentence **best** fit?

   f.   right after sentence 7
   g.   right after sentence 12
   h.   right after sentence 9
   j.   right after sentence 10

11. Choose the correct way to write the underlined part of sentence 18.

   I think navigation maps are <u>usefuller than</u> topographical maps.

   a.   useful than
   b.   more useful than
   c.   usefullest
   d.   No change is needed.

Sabrina is in the fourth grade. Her teacher asked each student to read a biography and to summarize it. Sabrina read a biography of Jackie Robinson. She organized her notes and wrote a rough draft. Now she needs your help editing and revising it.

Here is Sabrina's rough draft. Read it and then answer questions 1–10.

---

(1) Jackie Robinson was a very famous baseball player. (2) He was the first black person to play in the modern major leagues. (3) His real name was Jack Roosevelt Robinson he was born in Cairo, Georgia. (4) He went to college at <u>the University of California He</u> played four different sports in college.

(5) Jackie Robinson joined the Brooklyn Dodgers. (6) In 1947, he joined the Dodgers. (7) <u>He plays</u> for them for ten years. (8) He started as a first baseman. (9) He was <u>even famouser</u> for playing second base. (10) Jackie was <u>a very good hitter runner and base stealer.</u> (11) He had good numbers.

(12) Jackie Robinson won many awards during his career. (13) In 1947, he won the "Rookie of the Year" Award. (14) In 1949, he won the "Most Valuable Player" Award. (15) He was <u>elekted</u> to the Baseball Hall of Fame in 1962.

---

1. Choose the correct way to write the underlined part of sentence 4.

   He went to college at <u>the University of California He</u> played four different sports in college.

   a. the University of California, He
   b. the University of California. He
   c. the University of California? He
   d. No change is needed.

2. Choose the topic sentence of this composition.

   f. Jackie Robinson won many awards during his career.
   g. Jackie Robinson joined the Brooklyn Dodgers.
   h. He was the first black person to play in the modern major leagues.
   j. Jackie Robinson was a very famous baseball player.

3. Choose the correct way to write the underlined part of sentence 7.

   He plays for them for ten years.

   a. he plays
   b. His playing
   c. He played
   d. No change is needed.

4. Choose the sentence that is a supporting detail for the paragraph that begins with sentence 12.

   f. Jackie Robinson won many awards during his career.
   g. In 1947, he won the "Rookie of the Year" Award.
   h. He had good numbers.
   j. He started as a first baseman.

5. Choose the correct way to write the underlined part of sentence 9.

   He was even famouser for playing second base.

   a. the famousest
   b. even more famous
   c. most famouser
   d. No change is needed.

6. Choose the correct way to write the underlined part of sentence 10.

   Jackie was a very good hitter runner and base stealer.

   f. a very good hitter, runner, and base stealer.
   g. a very, good hitter, runner and base stealer.
   h. a very good hitter runner, and base stealer.
   j. No change is needed.

7. Sabrina wants to change sentence 11 so that it is more specific.

   He had good numbers.

   Choose the **best** way to rewrite the sentence.

   a. His batting average was good over his lifetime.
   b. He had a great lifetime batting average.
   c. He had a great lifetime batting average of .311.
   d. He had good batting averages.

8. Choose the **best** way to combine the ideas in sentences 5 and 6 into one sentence.

   Jackie Robinson joined the Brooklyn Dodgers. In 1947, he joined the Dodgers.

   f. Jackie Robinson joined the Brooklyn Dodgers in 1947.
   g. Jackie Robinson joined the Brooklyn Dodgers and then in 1947, he joined the Dodgers.
   h. Jackie Robinson joined 1947 with the Brooklyn Dodgers.
   j. Jackie Robinson was a Brooklyn Dodger in 1947.

9. Choose the correct way to write the underlined part of sentence 15.

   He was <u>elekted</u> to the Baseball Hall of Fame in 1962.

   a. ellected
   b. alected
   c. elected
   d. No change is needed.

10. Read sentence 3. It is poorly written.

His real name was Jack Roosevelt Robinson he was born in Cairo, Georgia.

Choose the **best** way to rewrite the sentence.

f. His real name was Jack Roosevelt Robinson. He was born in Cairo, Georgia.

g. His real name was Jack Roosevelt Robinson since he was born in Cairo, Georgia.

h. His real name was Jack Roosevelt Robinson, he was born in Cairo, Georgia.

j. His real name was Jack Roosevelt Robinson because he was born in Cairo, Georgia.

Izzy is in the fourth grade. His class read the book, *Morning Girl*, by Michael Dorris. It is about a sister and brother growing up on an island in the Bahamas in 1492. His teacher asked each student to imagine that she or he was the girl or boy in the story and to describe life on the island. Izzy wrote a rough draft. Now he needs your help editing and revising it.

Here is Izzy's rough draft. Read it and then answer questions 1–10.

(1) They call me "Star Boy." (2) I wish my sister understood me. (3) I hate being <u>bord.</u> (4) You know, I hate going to sleep at night. (5) My mom and dad call me "the bat that sleeps during the day." (6) My sister can't stand it. (7) She always <u>complain</u> about me. (8) She says I'm too noisy and too busy. (9) I like to say that I'm an expert on the stars. (10) I like to say that I know everything about the stars.

(11) Sometimes people bother me. (12) I don't like it when my friend laughs at me. (13) Today he called me "a mouse that chews on bark." (14) Dude, that is like, so rude.

(15) Sometimes I like to go to the beach by myself. (16) I like to pretend that I'm a rock. (17) <u>I curl up next to the real rocks. and</u> I don't move. (18) Nobody knows that <u>I'm their</u>, but I can hear everything. (19) I can feel everything, too. (20) I can feel the sun in the sky. (21) And the wind in the air.

(22) Sometimes I like a big storm. (23) Yesterday, I swam to the little island where only birds live. (24) There was a storm which I had to hold onto a tree. (25) I was scared, but sometimes it's fun to be scared. (26) If my mom and dad found out, <u>I'm be</u> in big trouble!

1. Choose the correct way to write the underlined part of sentence 3.

   I hate being <u>bord.</u>

   a. bored.
   b. board.
   c. borred.
   d. No change is needed.

60

2. Which one of these is **not** a complete sentence?

    f. And the wind in the air.
    g. Sometimes people bother me.
    h. Sometimes I like a big storm.
    j. I wish my sister understood me.

3. Choose the correct way to write the underlined part of sentence 7.

    She always <u>complain</u> about me.

    a. complaining
    b. complains
    c. do complain
    d. No change is needed.

4. Choose the **best** way to combine the ideas in sentences 9 and 10 into one sentence.

    I like to say that I'm an expert on the stars. I like to say that I know everything about the stars.

    f. I like to say that I'm an expert on the stars and also, I like to say that I know everything about the stars.
    g. I like to know everything there is to know about the stars and say I do.
    h. I like to be an expert and know everything about the stars.
    j. I like to say that I'm an expert and know everything about the stars.

5. Choose the correct way to write the underlined part of sentence 17.

    <u>**I curl up next to the real rocks. and** </u>**I don't move.**

    a. I curl up next to the real rocks, And
    b. I curl up next to the real rocks. And
    c. I curl up next to the real rocks, and
    d. No change is needed.

6. Choose the **best** way to write sentence 14 so that the composition maintains a consistent tone.

   Dude, that is like, so rude.

   f. I mean, that's rude, you know?
   g. That's not a very kind thing to say.
   h. That is, like, totally unfair.
   j. I'm not sure if that's rude.

7. Choose the correct way to write the underlined part of sentence 18.

   Nobody knows that <u>I'm their</u>, but I can hear everything.

   a. I'm they're
   b. Im their
   c. I'm there
   d. No change is needed.

8. Read sentence 24. It is poorly written.

   There was a storm which I had to hold onto a tree.

   Choose the **best** way to rewrite this sentence.

   f. A storm came up and I had to hold onto a tree.
   g. There was a storm so that I had to hold onto a tree.
   h. A storm came up and I had a tree.
   j. I held onto the tree for the storm.

9. Choose the correct way to write the underlined part of sentence 26.

   If my mom and dad found out, <u>I'm be</u> in big trouble!

   a. I'ld be
   b. I'd be
   c. I's be
   d. No change is needed.

10. Choose the sentence that is a supporting detail for the paragraph that begins with sentence 22.

    f.   You know, I hate going to sleep at night.

    g.   Today he called me "a mouse that chews on bark."

    h.   Yesterday, I swam to the little island where only birds live.

    j.   And the wind in the air.

Patrick's fourth-grade class is learning about the respiratory system. His teacher asked each student to imagine being an oxygen molecule and to write about his or her journey through the respiratory system. Patrick took notes and made an outline with his science partner. Then he wrote his rough draft. Now he needs your help editing and revising it.

Here is Patrick's rough draft. Read it and then answer questions 1–10.

(1) I am an oxygen molecule. (2) <u>Im made</u> of two oxygen atoms put together. (3) Molecules like me make up twenty percent of the air. (4) Here is my adventure in a human body. (5) We studied the human body in school this year.

(6) First, the human breathes in. (7) This is called "inspiration." (8) This person's breathing is very fast. (9) I think he is exercising. (10) I get pulled in <u>thru the nose.</u> (11) I travel down the long windpipe and I come to a fork in the road and I take the left "bronchus" into the left lung.

(12) The bronchus makes branches just like a tree. (13) I travel through smaller and smaller "bronchioles." (14) At the end of the last one, there are the "alveoli." (15) The alveoli are bunches of grapes. (16) In the alveoli <u>there is tiny blood vessels.</u> (17) They are called "pulmonary capillaries." (18) Here is where I meet a red blood cell. (19) This is the place where I get attached to a red blood cell.

(20) The red blood cell has molecules of hemoglobin in it. (21) A hemoglobin molecule picks me up <u>and carry me.</u> (22) First. (23) We go to the heart. (24) The heart pumps us to the body. (25) My blood cell goes to the right foot. (26) That's where I <u>finely</u> get dropped off!

1. Choose the correct way to write the underlined part of sentence 2.

    <u>Im made</u> of two oxygen atoms put together.

    a. I'am made
    b. Im' made
    c. I'm made
    d. No change is needed.

2. Choose the **best** way to combine the ideas in sentences 22 and 23 into one sentence.

   First. We go to the heart.

   f. First to the heart.
   g. First! We go to the heart.
   h. First, we go to the heart.
   j. The heart is the first.

3. Choose the correct way to write the underlined part of sentence 10.

   I get pulled in <u>thru the nose.</u>

   a. threw the nose.
   b. through the nose.
   c. though the nose.
   d. No change is needed.

4. Choose the sentence that does **not** belong in the paragraph that begins with sentence 1.

   f. sentence 4
   g. sentence 3
   h. sentence 2
   j. sentence 5

5. Choose the correct way to write the underlined part of sentence 16.

   In the alveoli <u>there is tiny blood vessels.</u>

   a. there are tiny blood vessels.
   b. there be tiny blood vessels.
   c. there was tiny blood vessels.
   d. No change is needed.

6. Read sentence 15. It is poorly written.

   The alveoli are bunches of grapes.

   Choose the **best** way to rewrite this sentence.

   f. The alveoli look like bunches of grapes.
   g. The alveoli are very similar in that they look like grapes.
   h. Alveoli and grapes are the same.
   j. Alveoli and grapes are two things that look alike.

7. Choose the correct way to write the underlined part of sentence 21.

   A hemoglobin molecule picks me up <u>and carry me.</u>

   a. and carried me.
   b. and carrying me.
   c. and carries me.
   d. No change is needed.

8. Read sentence 11. It is poorly written.

   **I travel down the long windpipe and I come to a fork in
   the road and I take the left "bronchus" into the left lung.**

   Choose the **best** way to rewrite the sentence.

   f. I travel down the long windpipe and then I come to a fork in the road and
       then I take the left "bronchus" into the left lung.
   g. I travel down the long windpipe. When I come to a fork in the road, I take
       the left "bronchus" into the left lung.
   h. I travel down the long windpipe, I come to a fork in the road, I take the left
       "bronchus" into the left lung.
   j. I travel down the long windpipe. I come to a fork in the road. I take the left
       "bronchus" into the left lung.

9. Choose the correct way to write the underlined part of sentence 26.

    That's where I <u>finely</u> get dropped off!

    a. finaly
    b. finally
    c. finelly
    d. No change is needed.

10. Choose the **best** way to combine the ideas in sentences 18 and 19 into one sentence.

    Here is where I meet a red blood cell. This is the place where I get attached to a red blood cell.

    f. This is the place where I meet and get attached to a red blood cell.
    g. Here is where I meet a red blood cell and this is also the place where I get attached to a red blood cell.
    h. Here is where I meet a red blood cell because this is the place where I get attached to a red blood cell.
    j. This is the place where we meet.

Margaret's fourth-grade class is studying the lives of the presidents of the United States. Her teacher asked each student to choose one president and to write a short biography of his life. Margaret chose to write about Dwight D. Eisenhower. She took notes from her books and wrote her rough draft. Now she needs your help editing and revising it.

Here is Margaret's rough draft. Read it and then answer questions 1–11.

(1) Dwight D. Eisenhower was a very popular and admired U.S. president. (2) He was born in texas in 1890. (3) His family grew vegetables on a farm. (4) Everybody thought that his brother, Edgar, was going to become the president.

(5) Dwight Eisenhower decided to become a soldier. (6) His parents didn't like that idea. (7) They were against war, but they let him to go to military school. (8) First, he learned how to be a soldier. (9) Then, being an army leader is what he learned to do next. (10) My brother, Jack, is in the army right now.

(11) Eisenhower taught soldiers how to use tanks in the First World War. (12) He became an advisor after that, and many army people came to him for help. (13) World War II broke out in 1939 Eisenhower was a great army leader during this war. (14) He went to Washington and organized many attacks. (15) He was very good at getting people to work together.

(16) In 1952, many people wanted Eisenhower to be the next president. (17) He didn't want to do it because he didt think a military person should be the president. (18) He changed his mind, tho, and he was elected president in 1952. (19) He was upset when the Russians put the first satellite into space, and he spends a lot of money to make our space program the best one in the world. (20) He was president until 1961. (21) He was president for two terms.

1. Choose the correct way to write the underlined part of sentence 2.

    He was born in texas in 1890.

    a. he was born in texas
    b. He was born in, texas
    c. He was born in Texas
    d. No change is needed.

68

2. Choose the topic sentence of this composition.

    f. He was very good at getting people to work together.

    g. He was president until 1961.

    h. He became an advisor after that, and many army people came to him for help.

    j. Dwight D. Eisenhower was a very popular and admired U.S. president.

3. Choose the correct way to write the underlined part of sentence 7.

They were against <u>war, but</u> they let him to go to military school.

    a. war. But

    b. war and

    c. war, but,

    d. No change is needed.

4. Read sentence 9. It is poorly written.

Then, being an army leader is what he learned to do next.

Choose the **best** way to rewrite this sentence.

    f. Then he was leader in army.

    g. Then, he learned how to be an army leader.

    h. Then, he learned how an army leader is.

    j. Then, being an army leader is what happened next.

5. Choose the correct way to write the underlined part of sentence 13.

   World War II broke out <u>in 1939 Eisenhower</u> was a great army leader during this war.

   a. in 1939, Eisenhower,
   b. in 1939. Eisenhower
   c. on 1939 Eisenhower
   d. No change is needed.

6. Choose the sentence that does **not** belong in the paragraph that begins with sentence 5.

   f. sentence 6
   g. sentence 8
   h. sentence 10
   j. sentence 9

7. Choose the correct way to write the underlined part of sentence 17.

   He didn't want to do it because he <u>didt</u> think a military person should be the president.

   a. didn't
   b. did not
   c. didint
   d. No change is needed.

8. Choose the **best** way to combine the ideas in sentences 20 and 21 into one sentence.

   He was president until 1961. He was president for two terms.

   f. He was president twice in 1961.
   g. He was the president for two terms in 1961.
   h. He was president for two terms in 1961.
   j. He was president for two terms, until 1961.

9. Choose the correct way to write the underlined part of sentence 18.

He changed his mind, <u>tho,</u> and he was elected president in 1952.

a. through,
b. thogh,
c. though,
d. No change is needed.

10. Choose the sentence that is NOT a supporting detail for the paragraph that begins with sentence 11.

f. Eisenhower taught soldiers how to use tanks in the First World War.
g. He became an advisor after that, and many army people came to him for help.
h. Then, being an army leader is what he learned to do next.
j. He was very good at getting people to work together.

11. Choose the correct way to write the underlined part of sentence 19.

He was upset when the Russians put the first satellite into space, and he <u>spends</u> a lot of money to make our space program the best one in the world.

a. spended
b. spent
c. spending
d. No change is needed.

Monica is in the fourth grade. Her class is learning about myths. Her teacher asked each student to choose one animal and to write a myth explaining how it acquired one of its traits. Monica chose to write about how the spider got its eight legs. She brainstormed her ideas and wrote an outline, and then she wrote her rough draft. Now she needs your help editing and revising it.

Here is Monica's rough draft. Read it and then answer questions 1–11.

(1) Once upon a time, the spiders on the earth walked on six legs just like insects do. (2) One day, there was <u>a spider named Gisela Gisela thought</u> she was better than everyone else. (3) She made the nicest webs and she had <u>the most pretty</u> eyes. (4) It made her mad that she only had six legs.

(5) One day, Gisela sitting in the center of her web. (6) Suddenly, a centipede walked by. (7) "Wow!" Gisela shouted, "I want to have <u>one hundred legs, to!</u>" (8) As soon as she said that, she heard, "Poof!" (9) Appeared her fairy godmother. (10) Cinderella also had a fairy godmother.

(11) "My dear child, your wish is granted!" said her fairy godmother. (12) Gisela looked down and she had one hundred legs!

(13) "Oh, boy, this is great, I can run as fast as a centipede now!" (14) She tried to run. (15) She <u>couldnt</u> even walk! (16) Her legs got caught in the web. (17) She was a mess. (18) All of the insects started laughing at her and she started crying.

(19) "Fairy godmother! (20) Fairy godmother! (21) Help! There's been a <u>mistak</u>!" she cried. (22) Her fairy godmother appeared again.

(23) "You have learned a good lesson, my Gisela. (24) It is not always better to have more you don't have to have one hundred legs, but from now on, all spiders will have eight legs. (25) That way, no one will ever forget this lesson."

(26) Now you know how the spider got <u>their</u> eight legs!

1. Choose the correct way to write the underlined part of sentence 2.

One day, there was <u>a spider named Gisela Gisela thought</u> she was better than everyone else.

a. a spider named Gisela? Gisela thought
b. a spider named Gisela. Gisela thought
c. a spider named Gisela, Gisela thought
d. No change is needed.

2. Read sentence 9. It is poorly written.

Appeared her fairy godmother.

Choose the **best** way to rewrite this sentence.

f. Her fairy godmother appeared.
g. Her fairy grandmother appeared.
h. Her fairy godmother made an appearance.
j. Appearing was her fairy godmother.

3. Choose the correct way to write the underlined part of sentence 3.

She made the nicest webs and she had <u>the most pretty</u> eyes.

a. the prettier
b. the more pretty
c. the prettiest
d. No change is needed.

4. Read sentence 24. It is poorly written.

It is not always better to have more you don't have to have one hundred legs, but from now on, all spiders will have eight legs.

Choose the **best** way to rewrite the sentence.

f. It is not always better to have more because you don't have to have one hundred legs, but from now on, all spiders will have eight legs.
g. It is not always better to have more and you don't have to have one hundred legs, but from now on, all spiders will have eight legs.
h. It is not always better to have more, you don't have to have one hundred legs, but from now on, all spiders will have eight legs.
j. It is not always better to have more. You don't have to have one hundred legs. From now on, all spiders will have eight legs.

5. Choose the correct way to write the underlined part of sentence 7.

   "Wow!" Gisela shouted, "I want to have <u>one hundred legs, to!</u>"

   a. one hundred legs, two!
   b. one hundred legs to!
   c. one hundred legs, too!
   d. No change is needed.

6. Choose the correct way to write the underlined part of sentence 5.

   One day, <u>Gisela sitting in the center</u> of her web.

   Which of these is the **best** way to rewrite it?

   f. Gisela sitting in the senter
   g. Gisela was sitting in the center
   h. Gisela had sat in the center
   j. No change is needed.

7. Choose the correct way to write the underlined part of sentence 15.

   She <u>couldnt</u> even walk!

   a. couldn't
   b. coul'dnt
   c. couldnt'
   d. No change is needed.

8. Choose the sentence that does **not** belong in the paragraph that begins with sentence 5.

   f. sentence 6
   g. sentence 8
   h. sentence 10
   j. sentence 7

9. Choose the correct way to write the underlined part of sentence 21.

   . . . There's been a <u>mistak</u>!" she cried.

   a. misteak
   b. mistake
   c. misstake
   d. No change is needed.

10. Monica wants to change sentence 16 so that it is more specific.

    Her legs got caught in the web.

    Choose the **best** way to rewrite the sentence.

    f. Her one hundred legs were tangled up.
    g. The web was so sticky that she got caught.
    h. She got badly stuck by her one hundred legs in the stickiness of the web.
    j. Her one hundred legs got all tangled up in the sticky web.

11. Choose the correct way to write the underlined part of sentence 26.

    Now you know how the spider got <u>their</u> eight legs!

    a. its
    b. they
    c. it's
    d. No change is needed.

Michael is in the fourth grade. His teacher asked each student to choose a famous person from history and to write a report about him or her. Michael chose to write about the life of Nathan Hale. He wrote a rough draft, but now he needs your help to edit and revise his work.

Here is Michael's rough draft. Read it and then answer questions 1–11.

(1) Nathan Hale was a hero in the American Revolutionary War. (2) Nathan Hale was born in <u>Coventry Connecticut</u> in 1755. (3) His parents raised a large family. (4) There was a lot of work to do on their farm, and Nathan grew very strong. (5) He <u>loved to run, leap wrestle throw, and play football.</u> (6) I made the football team this year!

(7) <u>Nathan liked to study, and they did well</u> in school. (8) He went to Yale College when he was fourteen years old. (9) Very popular student there.

(10) In 1773, Nathan graduated from Yale. (11) After that, he taught school for a few months. (12) <u>Schools were very simple</u> then. (13) They didn't even have blackboards! (14) Next, he got a job. (15) Nathan loved to teach.

(16) Soon, the Revolutionary War broke out. (17) This changed Nathan's <u>wole</u> life. (18) He joined Washington's army to fight the British. (19) He was a <u>brave Soldier</u> and captain. (20) The men in his regiment were discouraged because they were losing in New York. (21) He told them not give up. (22) He told them that they had to stay strong and brave for the country.

(23) Washington decided that he needed a spy. (24) Spies were important during the war, but nobody liked being a spy. (25) If a spy got caught, the punishment was death. (26) Nathan's friend told him not to do it that did not stop Nathan. (27) He went straight into the British camp. (28) He pretended that he was a teacher looking for work. (29) Unfortunately, he was caught before he made it back.

(30) Just before he was hanged by the British, <u>he says,</u> "I only regret that I have but one life to lose for my country." (31) These words are very famous now. (32) We will always remember Nathan Hale for his incredible bravery.

1. Choose the correct way to write the underlined part of sentence 2.

   Nathan Hale was born in <u>Coventry Connecticut</u> in 1755.

   a. coventry Connecticut,
   b. Coventry connecticut
   c. Coventry, Connecticut,
   d. No change is needed.

2. Michael wants to change sentence 14 so that it is more specific.

   Next, he <u>got a job.</u>

   Choose the **best** way to rewrite the underlined part of the sentence.

   f. worked as a master in New London, Connecticut.
   g. got a job in a school in New London, Connecticut.
   h. became a master of New London, Connecticut.
   j. got a job as a master of a school in New London, Connecticut.

3. Choose the correct way to write the underlined part of sentence 5.

   He <u>loved to run, leap wrestle throw, and play football.</u>

   a. loved to run, leap, wrestle, throw, and play football.
   b. loved to run leap wrestle throw and play football.
   c. loved to run, and leap, and wrestle, and throw, and play football.
   d. No change is needed.

4. Which one of these is **not** a complete sentence?

   f. Very popular student there.
   g. Nathan loved to teach.
   h. Soon, the Revolutionary War broke out.
   j. These words are very famous now.

5. Choose the correct way to write the underlined part of sentence 7.

   Nathan liked to study, and they did well in school.

   a. Nathan liked to study, and it did well
   b. Nathan liked to study, and he did well
   c. Nathan liked to study, and we did well
   d. No change is needed.

6. Choose the correct way to write the underlined part of sentence 12.

   Schools were very simple then.

   f. Schools are very simple
   g. Schools was very simple
   h. School were very simple
   j. No change is needed.

7. Choose the sentence that does **not** belong in the paragraph that begins with sentence 1.

   a. sentence 3
   b. sentence 2
   c. sentence 6
   d. sentence 5

8. Choose the correct way to write the underlined part of sentence 17.

   This changed Nathan's wole life.

   f. hole
   g. whole
   h. whol
   j. No change is needed.

9. Choose the correct way to write the underlined part of sentence 19.

    He was a <u>brave Soldier</u> and captain.

    a. Brave Soldier
    b. Brave soldier
    c. brave soldier
    d. No change is needed.

10. Choose the correct way to write the underlined part of sentence 30.

    Just before he was hanged by the British, <u>he says</u>, "I only regret that I have but one life to lose for my country."

    f. he said,
    g. he goes,
    h. he shouts,
    j. No change is needed.

11. Read sentence 26. It is poorly written.

    Nathan's friend told him not to do it that did not stop Nathan.

    Choose the **best** way to rewrite this sentence.

    a. Nathan's friend told him not to do it, that did not stop Nathan.
    b. Nathan's friend told him not to do it. That did not stop Nathan.
    c. Nathan's friend told him. Not to do it. That did not stop Nathan.
    d. Nathan had a friend who told him not to do it, but Nathan didn't listen to him and he did it anyway.

Hannah's fourth-grade class is learning about rocks and minerals. Her teacher asked each student to choose a rock or mineral and to write about it. Hannah chose to write about the mineral, graphite. She took notes, organized them, and wrote her rough draft. Now she needs your help editing and revising it.

Here is part of Hannah's rough draft. Read it and then answer questions 1–10.

(1) Minerals are very common <u>materiels</u> on earth. (2) They are what rocks are made of. (3) Minerals are in the sand, too. (4) They can even be found in places besides earth. (5) Graphite <u>was</u> a mineral. (6) There is a graphite mine in Texas.

(7) Graphite is one of the most common minerals in the world. (8) It is a black and greasy mineral. (9) Did you know that the lead in your pencil is not really lead? (10) It is really graphite. (11) The word, "graphite," comes from <u>the greek</u> word that means "to write." (12) To make pencils, graphite gets hardened and mixed with clay.

(13) Graphite is a very good conductor of electricity. (14) It can be used where very high voltage is instead of metal. (15) Graphite is hard to burn. (16) <u>Its good</u> for making melting pots. (17) It is good for making containers that hold strong acid. (18) It is used in nuclear reactors. (19) Graphite <u>is an very useful</u> mineral.

1. Hannah wants to change sentence 4 so that it is more specific.

   They can even be found <u>in places besides earth</u>.

   Choose the **best** way to rewrite the underlined part of the sentence.

   a. on some other different planets
   b. in outer space
   c. on Mercury, Mars, and Venus
   d. beyond the great beyond

2. Choose the correct way to write sentence 5.

   Graphite was a mineral.

   f. Graphite is a mineral.
   g. Graphite will be a mineral.
   h. Graphite were a mineral.
   j. No change is needed.

3. Hannah wants to add this sentence to the paragraph that begins with sentence 1.

   However, most of our graphite comes from Mexico.

   Where would the sentence **best** fit?

   a. right after sentence 1
   b. right after sentence 2
   c. right after sentence 4
   d. right after sentence 6

4. Choose the correct way to write the underlined part of sentence 11.

   The word, "graphite," comes from <u>the greek</u> word that means "to write."

   f. the Greek
   g. The Greek
   h. the GREEK
   j. No change is needed.

5. Read sentence 14. It is poorly written.

    It can be used where very high voltage is instead of metal.

    Choose the **best** way to rewrite this sentence.

    a. It can be used instead of metal where there is very high voltage.
    b. It can be used when very high voltage, there is that instead of metal.
    c. It can be used. When very high voltage is instead of metal.
    d. It can be used instead of metal, and very high voltage is.

6. Choose the correct way to write the underlined part of sentence 19.

    Graphite <u>is an very useful</u> mineral.

    f. is a/an useful
    g. is an useful
    h. is a very useful
    j. No change is needed.

7. Choose the **best** way to combine the ideas in sentences 16 and 17 into one sentence.

    <u>Its good </u>for making melting pots. It is good for making containers that hold strong acid.

    a. It is good for making melting pots. It is good for a lot of things. And containers that hold strong acid.
    b. It is good for making things. It is good for making things like melting pots and for making things like containers that hold strong acid.
    c. It is good for making melting pots, good for making containers. Things that hold strong acid.
    d. It is good for making melting pots and containers that hold strong acid.

8. Choose the correct way to write the underlined part of sentence 1.

   Minerals are very common <u>materiels</u> on earth.

   f. material
   g. materiales
   h. materials
   j. No change is needed.

9. Choose the topic sentence for the paragraph that begins with sentence 13.

   a. Graphite is a very good conductor of electricity.
   b. It can be used where very high voltage is instead of metal.
   c. Graphite is hard to burn.
   d. Graphite <u>is an very useful</u> mineral.

10. Choose the correct way to write the underlined part of sentence 16.

   <u>Its good </u>for making melting pots.

   f. Its' good
   g. It's good
   h. Its's good
   j. No change is needed.

Nick's fourth-grade class is studying the climatic regions of the world. Nick's teacher asked each student to choose one country in a dry climatic region and to describe how the climate has affected life in that country. Nick chose to write about Libya. He took notes at the library, organized them, and wrote his rough draft. Now he needs your help editing and revising it.

Here is Nick's rough draft. Read it and then answer questions 1–11.

---

(1) Libya is in northern Africa. (2) The Sahara <u>dessert</u> covers ninety-five percent of its land. (3) This has affected Libya in many ways.

(4) The desert is a hard place to live. (5) Huge sand dunes cover a lot of the land. (6) The <u>tempatures</u> get very hot during the day and cool at night. (7) Libya's desert gets less than two inches of rainfall per year it is impossible to farm there. (8) Libya must import most of the food that it needs.

(9) Libya's people live mostly along the coast of the <u>mediterranean sea.</u> (10) This coastal area gets about sixteen inches of rainfall per year.

(11) Some people live in oases. (12) An "oasis" an area in the desert where underground water comes to the surface. (13) It is a place where plants can grow and animals can live.

(14) Libya used to be a very poor country because of its bad climate. (15) Many people survived on small family farms, but only five percent of the land was useful. (16) Then, in 1959, oil was discovered. (17) This has changed <u>the country's whole economy.</u> (18) Most of Canada's oil lies in Alberta. (19) Today, Libya is <u>one of the most rich</u> countries in the world.

---

1. Choose the topic sentence for the paragraph that begins with sentence 4.

   a. The desert is a hard place to live.
   b. Huge sand dunes cover a lot of the land.
   c. Libya's desert gets less than two inches of rainfall per year it is impossible to farm there.
   d. Libya must import most of the food that it needs.

2. Choose the correct way to write the underlined part of sentence 2.

The Sahara <u>dessert</u> covers ninety-five percent of its land.

f. deserrt

g. desssert

h. desert

j. No change is needed.

3. Read sentence 7. It is poorly written.

Libya's desert gets less than two inches of rainfall per year it is impossible to farm there.

Choose the **best** way to rewrite the sentence.

a. Libya's desert gets less than two inches of rainfall per year because it is impossible to farm there.

b. Libyas desert gets less than two inches of rainfall per year, it is impossible to farm there.

c. Libya's desert gets less than two inches of rainfall, impossible to farm there.

d. Libya's desert gets less than two inches of rainfall per year, so it is impossible to farm there.

4. Choose the correct way to write the underlined part of sentence 19.

Today, Libya is <u>one of the most rich</u> countries in the world.

f. one of the most richest

g. one of the richest

h. one of the richiest

j. No change is needed.

5. Choose the correct way to write the underlined part of sentence 9.

   Libya's people live mostly along the coast of the <u>mediterranean sea.</u>

   a. Mediterranean Sea.
   b. Mediterranean sea.
   c. mediterranean Sea.
   d. No change is needed.

6. Nick wants to add this sentence either to the paragraph that begins with sentence 9 or the paragraph that begins with sentence 11.

   Since this part of the country is close to the sea, it has warm summers and mild winters.

   Where would the sentence **best** fit?

   f. right after sentence 12
   g. right after sentence 11
   h. right after sentence 13
   j. right after sentence 9

7. Choose the correct way to write the underlined part of sentence 17.

   This has changed <u>the country's whole economy.</u>

   a. the countrys' whole economy.
   b. the countries' whole economy.
   c. the countries whole economy.
   d. No change is needed.

86

8. Choose the sentence that does **not** belong in the paragraph that begins with sentence 14.

    f.   sentence 19
    g.   sentence 15
    h.   sentence 16
    j.   sentence 18

9. Choose the correct way to write the underlined part of sentence 6.

The <u>tempatures</u> get very hot during the day and cool at night.

    a.   tempetures
    b.   temperatures
    c.   temperachors
    d.   No change is needed.

10. Which one of these is **not** a complete sentence?

    f.   This has affected Libya in many ways.
    g.   It is a place where plants can grow and animals can live.
    h.   An "oasis" an area in the desert where underground water comes to the surface.
    j.   Then, in 1959, oil was discovered.

11. Choose the sentence that **best** fits right after sentence 16.

    a.   Most Libyan people are Muslim.
    b.   Tripoli is the capital of Libya, and almost two million people live there.
    c.   Experts think that there are about twenty-three billion barrels of oil in Libya.
    d.   All Libyan people can vote at the age of eighteen.

Marcus's fourth-grade class is studying volcanoes. His teacher asked each student to research one volcano in history and then to write a short report. Marcus took notes at the library and put his ideas into a graphic organizer. Then he wrote his rough draft, and now he needs your help editing and revising it.

Here is Marcus's rough draft. Read it and then answer questions 1–10.

(1) Did you know that there was a volcanic eruption in the United States? (2) In 1980, ninety-five miles south of <u>seattle, Washington,</u> Mount Saint Helens erupted. (3) The eruption was a violent one. (4) Fifty-seven people lost their lives. (5) The mountain peak became one thousand feet shorter than it had been before.

(6) When Mount Saint Helens erupted, it caused great damage. (7) The volcano started forest fires. (8) It melted snow caused floods and mudslides. (9) Millions of trees were <u>flatened.</u> (10) <u>Buildings, roads and bridges</u> were washed away, and crops were destroyed. (11) Repairing the damage <u>will cost</u> hundreds of millions of dollars.

(12) In the past four thousand five hundred years, Mount Saint Helens has erupted many times. (13) However, it was inactive from 1852 to 1980. (14) That is why it surprised people. (15) Between 1980 and 1986, <u>they're</u> were many more eruptions, but these were small. (16) They did not cause any deaths they did not cause any great damage.

1. Choose the **best** way to combine the ideas in sentences 3 and 4 into one sentence.

   The eruption was a violent one. Fifty-seven people lost their lives.

   a. The eruption was a violent one fifty-seven people lost their lives.
   b. The eruption was a violent one, and fifty-seven people lost their lives.
   c. The eruption was a violent one, but fifty-seven people lost their lives.
   d. The eruption was, a violent one, fifty-seven people lost their lives.

2. Choose the correct way to write the underlined part of sentence 9.

    Millions of trees were <u>flatened.</u>

    f. flattenned.
    g. flattended.
    h. flattened.
    j. No change is needed.

3. Marcus wants to add this sentence to the paragraph that begins with sentence 1.

    A big crater was left at the top of the mountain.

    Where would the sentence **best** fit?

    a. right after sentence 1
    b. right after sentence 5
    c. right after sentence 3
    d. right after sentence 4

4. Choose the correct way to write the underlined part of sentence 10.

    <u>Buildings, roads and bridges</u> were washed away, and crops were destroyed.

    f. Buildings, roads, and bridges
    g. Buildings, roads, bridges
    h. Buildings and roads, and bridges
    j. No change is needed.

5. Choose the topic sentence for the paragraph that begins with sentence 6.

    a. When Mount Saint Helens erupted, it caused great damage.
    b. The volcano started forest fires.
    c. It melted snow caused floods and mudslides.
    d. Repairing the damage <u>will cost</u> hundreds of millions of dollars.

6. Choose the correct way to write the underlined part of sentence 2.

   In 1980, ninety-five miles south of <u>seattle, Washington,</u> Mount Saint Helens erupted.

   f. seattle, washington,
   g. Seattle, washington,
   h. Seattle, Washington,
   j. No change is needed.

7. Read sentence 8. It is poorly written.

   It melted snow caused floods and mudslides.

   Choose the **best** way to rewrite this sentence.

   a. It melted snow, floods and mudslides, which it caused.
   b. Caused floods and mudslides, it melted the snow.
   c. It melted the floods and mudslides with snow.
   d. It melted snow, causing floods and mudslides.

8. Choose the correct way to write the underlined part of sentence 15.

   Between 1980 and 1986, <u>they're</u> were many more eruptions, but these were small.

   f. their
   g. there
   h. ther'ye
   j. No change is needed.

9. Read sentence 16. It is poorly written.

    They did not cause any deaths they did not cause any great damage.

    Choose the **best** way to rewrite the sentence so that it does not repeat ideas.

    a. They did not cause any deaths, and they did not cause any great damage.
    b. They did not cause deaths, they did not cause great damage.
    c. They did not cause any deaths or they did not cause any great damage.
    d. They did not cause any deaths or great damage.

10. Choose the correct way to write the underlined part of sentence 11.

    Repairing the damage <u>will cost</u> hundreds of millions of dollars.

    f. costed
    g. cost
    h. had costed
    j. No change is needed.

Katherine is in the fourth grade. Her class is learning about bus safety. Her teacher asked each student to write a short report explaining what students could do to make bus rides safer. Katherine made an outline of her ideas, and then she wrote her rough draft. Now she needs your help editing and revising it.

Here is Katherine's rough draft. Read it and then answer questions 1–10.

(1) There are quite a few things that students can do to improve bus safety. (2) First of all, it <u>was</u> important to wait at the bus stop. (3) We shouldn't cross the street before our bus arrives. (4) We should also stand back from the curb. (5) Some drivers are not careful.

(6) When the bus arrives, we should carefully look before crossing the street. (7) <u>Car drivers doesn't</u> always remember to stop. (8) Sometimes they pass the bus on the right or left side. (9) Even when the red lights are flashing!

(10) Before we cross in front of the bus, we should make eye contact with the driver. (11) <u>The Driver</u> has to give us a signal to tell us that it's safe to cross. (12) We should never bend down in front of the school bus. (13) If we do, the driver will not be able to see us. (14) We should never turn back to get something we left on getting off the bus.

(15) On the bus, we should follow the <u>driver's directions</u>. (16) Also, on the bus we should not make a lot of noise. (17) If we bother the driver, then he or she won't be able to drive very well. (18) We should also respect other passengers. (19) Nobody likes being <u>bullyed</u> on the bus.

1. Katherine wants to change sentence 6 so that it is more specific.

   When the bus arrives, we should carefully <u>look</u> before crossing the street.

   Choose the **best** way to rewrite the underlined part of the sentence.

   a. look up and down the street
   b. look both ways
   c. look left, right, and left again
   d. look safely

    92

2. Choose the correct way to write the underlined part of sentence 2.

First of all, it <u>was</u> important to wait at the bus stop.

   f. is

   g. will be

   h. had been

   j. No change is needed.

3. Choose the **best** way to combine the ideas in sentences 15 and 16 into one sentence.

On the bus, we should follow the driver's directions. Also, on the bus we should not make a lot of noise.

   a. On the bus, we should follow the driver's directions, also, on the bus, we should not make a lot of noise.

   b. On the bus, we should follow the driver's directions and not make a lot of noise.

   c. On the bus, we should follow the driver's directions, or on the bus, we should not make a lot of noise.

   d. On the bus, we should follow the driver's directions, and on the bus, we should not make a lot of noise.

4. Choose the correct way to write the underlined part of sentence 11.

<u>The Driver</u> has to give us a signal to tell us that it's safe to cross.

   f. the Driver

   g. the driver

   h. The driver

   j. No change is needed.

5. Which one of these is **not** a complete sentence?

    a. We shouldn't cross the street before our bus arrives.
    b. Even when the red lights are flashing!
    c. We should never bend down in front of the school bus.
    d. If we bother the driver, then he or she won't be able to drive very well.

6. Choose the correct way to write the underlined part of sentence 19.

    Nobody likes being <u>bullyed</u> on the bus.

    f. bullyied
    g. bulleed
    h. bullied
    j. No change is needed.

7. Katherine wants to add this sentence to the paragraph that begins with sentence 15.

    We should never put our hands out of the window because a tree, pole, or truck might hit them.

    Where would the sentence **best** fit?

    a. right after sentence 16
    b. right after sentence 19
    c. right after sentence 18
    d. right after sentence 17

8. Choose the correct way to write the underlined part of sentence 15.

   On the bus, we should follow the <u>driver's directions.</u>

   f. drivers directions.
   g. drivers' directions.
   h. drivers's directions.
   j. No change is needed.

9. Read sentence 14. It is poorly written.

   We should never turn back to get something we left on getting off the bus.

   Choose the **best** way to rewrite this sentence.

   a. After getting off the bus, we should never turn back to get something we have left behind.
   b. We should never turn back getting something we left after getting off the bus.
   c. And we should never turn back off the bus to get something we left.
   d. We should never turn back anything to get off the bus.

10. Choose the correct way to write the underlined part of sentence 7.

   <u>Car drivers doesn't</u> always remember to stop.

   f. Car drivers didn't
   g. Car drivers don't
   h. Car drivers will have not
   j. No change is needed.

Austin's fourth-grade class is learning about the Bill of Rights. His teacher asked each student to choose one amendment from the Bill of Rights and to describe how it is important to the country. Austin brainstormed his ideas, organized them, and wrote his rough draft. Now he needs your help editing and revising it.

Here is Austin's rough draft. Read it and then answer questions 1–11.

(1) The Bill of Rights is a group of <u>Ten Amendments</u>. (2) They were added to the *Constitution of the United States*. (3) They were added in 1788. (4) France also has a Bill of Rights. (5) <u>Let me tell you</u> why the Sixth Amendment is important.

(6) The Sixth Amendment says that, when you are accused of a crime, you get a fair trial. (7) Not be held for a long time in prison without a trial. (8) It also means that you will get a fair jury. (9) The jury will be made up of people who do not <u>now</u> you. (10) They will not be people who already think that you are guilty. (11) This is really important the jury has to look at all of the facts and decide whether you are guilty or not guilty.

(12) The Sixth Amendment also says that you deserve to have an attorney to represent you. (13) <u>That mean</u> that you don't have to go through the trial all by yourself with no one to help you.

(14) I think the Sixth Amendment makes our country a fair place. (15) If someone says without any <u>prove</u> that you have committed a crime, you don't just go straight to jail.

1. Choose the **best** way to combine the ideas in sentences 2 and 3 into one sentence.

    They were added to the *Constitution of the United States*. They were added in 1788.

    a. They were added to the *Constitution of the United States* that was added in 1788.
    b. They were added to the *Constitution of the United States* being added in 1788.
    c. They were added to the *Constitution of the United States* in 1788.
    d. They were added to the *Constitution of the United States*, they were added in 1788.

2. Choose the correct way to write the underlined part of sentence 1.

    The Bill of Rights is a group of <u>Ten Amendments.</u>

    f.   10 Amendments.
    g.   ten amendments.
    h.   ten Amendements.
    j.   No change is needed.

3. Choose the sentence that does **not** belong in the paragraph that begins with sentence 1.

    a.   sentence 4
    b.   sentence 3
    c.   sentence 2
    d.   sentence 1

4. Choose the correct way to write the underlined part of sentence 13.

    <u>That mean</u> that you don't have to go through the trial all by yourself with no one to help you.

    f.   That will mean
    g.   That meaning
    h.   That means
    j.   No change is needed.

5. Choose the topic sentence for the paragraph that begins with sentence 6.

    a.   The Sixth Amendment says that, when you are accused of a crime, you get a fair trial.
    b.   Not be held for a long time in prison without a trial.
    c.   It also means that you will get a fair jury.
    d.   They will not be people who already think that you are guilty.

6. Choose the correct way to write the underlined part of sentence 15.

    If someone says without any <u>prove</u> that you have committed a crime, you don't just go straight to jail.

    f. proof
    g. proove
    h. pruff
    j. No change is needed.

7. Which one of these is **not** a complete sentence?

    a. They were added in 1788.
    b. Not be held for a long time in prison without a trial.
    c. It also means that you will get a fair jury.
    d. I think the Sixth Amendment makes our country a fair place.

8. Read sentence 11. It is poorly written.

    This is really important the jury has to look at all of the facts and decide whether you are guilty or not guilty.

    Choose the **best** way to rewrite the sentence.

    f. This is really important, the jury. To look at all of the facts and decide whether you are guilty or not guilty.

    g. Really important, the jury has to look at all of the facts, to decide whether you are guilty, or not guilty.

    h. This is really important. The jury has to look at all of the facts. And decide whether you are guilty or not guilty.

    j. This is really important because the jury has to look at all of the facts and decide whether you are guilty or not guilty.

9. Choose the correct way to write the underlined part of sentence 9.

   The jury will be made up of people who do not <u>now</u> you.

   a. no
   b. kno
   c. know
   d. No change is needed.

10. Choose the sentence that **best** fits right after sentence 13.

    f. The first eight amendments deal with the rights of every American citizen.
    g. Canada also has a Bill of Rights.
    h. If you are too poor to pay for an attorney, the state will give you one.
    j. The first amendment guarantees free speech.

11. Choose the correct way to write the underlined part of sentence 5.

    <u>Let me tell you</u> why the Sixth Amendment is important.

    a. Let's me tell you
    b. Lets me tell you
    c. Tell me
    d. No change is needed.

Jafar's fourth-grade class is learning about endangered species. His teacher asked each student to choose one endangered species, to explain why it is endangered, and to tell what is being done about it. Jafar chose to write about tigers. He wrote his rough draft, and now he needs your help editing and revising it.

Here is Jafar's rough draft. Read it and then answer questions 1–10.

(1) The tiger is a member of the cat family. (2) People are afraid of tigers, tigers sometimes kill and eat people. (3) However, they only do that when they are very hungry and <u>three</u> is no other food around. (4) Sometimes they do it <u>when they are not able</u> to go after their usual prey.

(5) Tigers are an endangered species. (6) There are eight kinds of tigers in the world. (7) Three kinds is already extinct. (8) Three kinds are endangered. (9) All the tigers might go extinct if we do not help them.

(10) Tigers are endangered because of what people do. (11) People cut down the trees in the <u>forrests</u> where tigers live. (12) This is called "clearing the forest." (13) People also move into areas where tigers used to live. (14) Another reason is "poaching" that the tigers are endangered. (15) Poaching is when people kill animals for money.

(16) Some countries are trying to save the tigers. (17) The South China tigers are endangered. (18) China passed the Wild Animal Protection Law in 1981 to try to save them. (19) Some <u>countries's</u> make nature preserves. (20) These are areas where hunting and clearing are not allowed. (21) Some countries raise tigers in zoos. (22) Tigers are easy to breed and raise in zoos. (23) Monkeys are easy to raise in the zoo, too.

(24) I hope we <u>don't</u> lose any more tigers. (25) Extinction is forever!

1. Jafar wants to add this sentence to the paragraph that begins with sentence 10.

   Poaching is still a big problem today.

   Where would the sentence **best** fit?

   a. right after sentence 10
   b. right after sentence 11
   c. right after sentence 13
   d. right after sentence 15

100

2. Choose the correct way to write the underlined part of sentence 7.

   Three kinds <u>is already</u> extinct.

   f. are already
   g. were already
   h. will already be
   j. No change is needed.

3. Jafar wants to change sentence 4 so that it is more specific.

   Sometimes they do it when <u>they are not able</u> to go after their usual prey.

   Choose the **best** way to rewrite the underlined part of the sentence.

   a. they can't
   b. they are too sick or hurt
   c. it's hard
   d. they have too much trouble

4. Choose the correct way to write the underlined part of sentence 11.

   People cut down the trees in the <u>forrests</u> where tigers live.

   f. forrest
   g. foresters
   h. forests
   j. No change is needed.

5. Read sentence 2. It is poorly written.

    People are afraid of tigers, tigers sometimes kill and eat people.

    Choose the **best** way to rewrite the sentence.

    a. People are afraid of tigers because tigers sometimes kill and eat people.
    b. People are afraid of tigers, sometimes killing and eating people.
    c. People are afraid of tigers sometimes they kill and eat people.
    d. People are afraid of tigers kill and eat people sometimes.

[Special Problems—there/they're/their]

6. Choose the correct way to write the underlined part of sentence 3.

    However, they only do that when they are very hungry and <u>three</u> is no other food around.

    f. they're
    g. there
    h. their
    j. No change is needed.

7. Read sentence 14. It is poorly written.

    Another reason is "poaching" that the tigers are endangered.

    Choose the **best** way to rewrite this sentence.

    a. Another reason that endangered are the tigers is "poaching."
    b. Another reason is "poaching" that the endangered tigers.
    c. Another reason is that the tigers are endangered.
    d. "Poaching" is another reason that the tigers are endangered.

8. Choose the correct way to write the underlined part of sentence 24.

   I hope we <u>don't</u> lose any more tigers.

   f. doesn't
   g. dont
   h. dont'
   j. No change is needed.

9. Choose the sentence that does **not** belong in the paragraph that begins with sentence 16.

   a. sentence 20
   b. sentence 21
   c. sentence 22
   d. sentence 23

10. Choose the correct way to write the underlined part of sentence 19.

   Some <u>countries's</u> make nature preserves.

   f. countriess'
   g. countries
   h. countries'
   j. No change is needed.

Vanessa's fourth-grade class is studying units of measurement. The teacher asked each student to invent a new unit of measurement, to describe it, and then to use it to measure several objects. Vanessa brainstormed with Miranda, her science partner. Then she wrote her rough draft. Now she needs your help editing and revising it.

Here is Vanessa's rough draft. Read it and then answer questions 1–10.

(1) Our new unit of measurement is a vanmir. (2) The name, "vanmir," comes from the first three letters in the names, "**Van**essa" and "**Mir**anda."

(3) One Vanmir equals the length of Vanessa's hand and the length of Miranda's hand put together. (4) We made a piece of paper one vanmir long. (5) We folded it again and in again half. (6) We opened up the piece of paper. (7) <u>We marking</u> the folds. (8) We made a <u>piece</u> of cardboard one vanmir long. (9) Then we put the paper next to the cardboard. (10) We marked the cardboard where there were folds in the paper. (11) Three marks and four sections. (12) That is how we made our vanmir.

(13) We measured some things in the classroom. (14) Our desks are two and one- half vanmirs wide. (15) These desks are better than the ones we had last year. (16) <u>Mirandas pencil</u> is exactly one-half of a vanmir long. (17) The flagpole is four and one-fourth vanmirs long. (18) The chalkboard is seven <u>vanmirs</u> wide.

(19) The vanmir was a good unit of <u>mesurement.</u> (20) It worked very well.

1. Read sentence 5. It is poorly written.

   We folded it again and in again half.

   Choose the **best** way to rewrite this sentence.

   a. We again folded half again.
   b. We folded it halfing and half again.
   c. We folded it in half, and then we folded it in half again.
   d. We half folded it, folding it in half once again.

2. Choose the correct way to write the underlined part of sentence 8.

   We made a <u>piece</u> of cardboard one vanmir long.

   f. peace
   g. peece
   h. peice
   j. No change is needed.

3. Choose the correct way to write the underlined part of sentence 16.

   <u>Mirandas pencil</u> is exactly one-half of a vanmir long.

   a. Miranda's pencil
   b. Mirandas' pencil
   c. Mirandas's pencil
   d. No change is needed.

4. Which one of these is **not** a complete sentence?

   f. We made a piece of paper one vanmir long.
   g. Three marks and four sections.
   h. The chalkboard is seven vanmirs wide.
   j. It worked very well.

5. Choose the correct way to write the underlined part of sentence 19.

   The vanmir was a good unit of <u>mesurement.</u>

   a. measurement.
   b. measurment.
   c. meshurment.
   d. No change is needed.

6. Choose the topic sentence for the paragraph that begins with sentence 3.

   f. We made a piece of paper one vanmir long.
   g. We folded it again and in again half.
   h. We opened up the piece of paper.
   j. That is how we made our vanmir.

7. Choose the correct way to write the underlined part of sentence 7.

   <u>We marking</u> the folds.

   a. We was marking
   b. We did mark
   c. We marked
   d. No change is needed.

8. Choose the sentence that does **not** belong in the paragraph that begins with sentence 13.

   f. sentence 13
   g. sentence 17
   h. sentence 15
   j. sentence 18

9. Choose the correct way to write the underlined part of sentence 18.

    The chalkboard is seven <u>vanmirs</u> wide.

    a. VanMirs
    b. Vanmirs
    c. vanMirs
    d. No change is needed.

10. Choose the sentence that **best** fits right after sentence 17.

    f. The teacher's cactus is two and one-half vanmirs tall.
    g. There are thirty-six inches in a yard.
    h. My bathtub at home is eight vanmirs long.
    j. It takes us fifteen steps to walk across the classroom.

Taylor's fourth grade reading class is studying the genre, "legends." A legend is a story that has been passed down through many generations but might not be completely true. Her teacher asked each student to read a legend and to summarize it. Taylor chose to write about the legend of Pocahontas. She wrote her rough draft, and now she needs your help editing and revising it.

Here is Taylor's rough draft. Read it and then answer questions 1–10.

(1) Pocahontas was born in 1595, and she was an Algonquin Native American princess. (2) Her father <u>were</u> Chief Powhatan. (3) There is an interesting legend about Pocahontas.

(4) In 1607, <u>the english captain,</u> John Smith, landed in America with some other people. (5) They wanted to start a new colony that they would call "Jamestown," in honor of the English king, James I. (6) John Smith started exploring the area with his fellow Englishmen. (7) When Pocahontas met them, she liked John Smith the best.

(8) The Native Americans captured John Smith and brought him to Chief Powhatan's house. (9) At first, they were very nice to him. (10) They gave him a great feast. (11) Then, they grabbe him and stretched him over some big rocks. (12) The Native Americans looked like <u>their</u> ready to beat him. (13) Suddenly, <u>Pocahontas runs to him</u> and put her head over his head so that he would not be killed. (14) Then she pulled him to his feet.

(15) Captain John Smith, Powhatan's friend and adopted son, he became. (16) Pocahontas visited Jamestown many times. (17) She helped make sure that the English <u>colonie</u> had everything it needed to survive. (18) Later, she traveled to England she represented the Native American people she helped the Native Americans and the English people to become friends.

1. Choose the topic sentence of this composition.

   a. Pocahontas was born in 1595, and she was an Algonquin Native American princess.
   b. There is an interesting legend about Pocahontas.
   c. When Pocahontas met them, she liked John Smith the best.
   d. Pocahontas visited Jamestown many times.

2. Choose the correct way to write the underlined part of sentence 4.

   In 1607, <u>the english captain,</u> John Smith, landed in America with some other people.

   f. the english Captain
   g. the English Captain
   h. the English captain
   j. No change is needed.

3. Choose the **best** way to combine the ideas in sentences 9 and 10 into one sentence.

   At first, they were very nice to him. They gave him a great feast.

   a. At first, they were very nice to him and gave him a great feast.
   b. At first, they were very nice to him gave him a great feast.
   c. At first, they were very nice to him, a great feast.
   d. At first, very nice they gave him a great feast.

4. Choose the correct way to write the underlined part of sentence 12.

   The Native Americans looked like <u>their</u> ready to beat him.

   f. they were
   g. there were
   h. thcy'rc
   j. No change is needed.

5. Choose the sentence that **best** fits right after sentence 12.

   a. The settlers were looking for gold in the New World.
   b. Jamestown was the first capital of Virginia.
   c. They stood over him, holding clubs.
   d. John Smith was born in Willoughby, England.

6. Read sentence 15. It is poorly written.

   Captain John Smith, Powhatan's friend and adopted son, he became.

   Choose the **best** way to rewrite the sentence.

   f. Captain John Smith and Powhatan's friend became his adopted son.
   g. Captain John Smith's Powhatan friend and adopted son became.
   h. Captain John Smith became Powhatan's adopted son's friend.
   j. Captain John Smith became Powhatan's friend and adopted son.

7. Choose the correct way to write the underlined part of sentence 13.

   Suddenly, <u>Pocahontas runs to him</u> and put her head over his head so that he would not be killed.

   a. Pocahontas was running to him
   b. Pocahontas will run to him
   c. Pocahontas ran to him
   d. No change is needed.

8. Choose the correct way to write the underlined part of sentence 2.

   Her father <u>were</u> Chief Powhatan.

   f. is
   g. was
   h. would be
   j. No change is needed.

9. Read sentence 18. It is poorly written.

Later, she traveled to England she represented the Native American people she helped the Native Americans and the English people to become friends.

Choose the **best** way to rewrite the sentence.

a. Later, she traveled to England, where she represented the Native American people. She helped the Native Americans and the English people to become friends.

b. Later, she traveled to England she represented the Native American people. She helped the Native Americans and the English people to become friends.

c. Later, traveling to England, represented the Native American people, helped the Native Americans, and the English people to become friends.

d. Later, she traveled to England. She represented the Native American people Native Americans and the English people become friends.

10. Choose the correct way to write the underlined part of sentence 17.

She helped make sure that the English <u>colonie</u> had everything it needed to survive.

f. colony
g. coloknee
h. coloney
j. no change

Barbara's fourth-grade class is learning about the states of matter. Her teachers asked each student to choose two states of matter and to describe their differences. Barbara chose to write about liquids and gases. She wrote her rough draft, and now she needs your help editing and revising it.

Here is Barbara's rough draft. Read it and then answer questions 1–11.

(1) Gases and liquids are both made of tiny things called "molecules." (2) Molecules are so tiny that we cannot see them they make up everything in the world. (3) However, <u>gases and liquids</u> are very different from each other.

(4) There is the molecules in a gas a lot of free space between. (5) Air is a gas. (6) The gas expands to fill a space. (7) The <u>molecules moves</u> very quickly. (8) They often bump into each other. (9) If the gas gets hot or if it gets <u>squeazed</u> into a smaller space, the molecules hit each other more often. (10) They can hit each other billions of times per second.

(11) The molecules in a liquid don't have much space between them. (12) They touch each other, but they are not attached even though they touch each other. (13) They can move freely and slide past each other. (14) Liquids change to fit the shape of its containers. (15) Impossible to squeeze a liquid into a smaller space. (16) This is because <u>the molecules were already</u> close together.

1. Read sentence 2. It is poorly written.

    **Molecules are so tiny that we cannot see them they
    make up everything in the world.**

    Choose the **best** way to rewrite the sentence.

    a. Molecules are so tiny they make up everything in the world that we cannot see.
    b. Molecules are so tiny that we cannot see them. Making up everything in the world.
    c. Molecules are so tiny. That we cannot see them they make up everything in the world.
    d. Molecules are so tiny that we cannot see them, but they make up everything in the world.

2. Choose the correct way to write the underlined part of sentence 7.

   The <u>molecules moves</u> very quickly.

   f. molecules move
   g. molecule moves
   h. molecules moving
   j. No change is needed.

3. Read sentence 4. It is poorly written.

   There is the molecules in a gas a lot of free space between.

   Choose the **best** way to rewrite this sentence.

   a. There is the molecules a lot of free space in a gas.
   b. There is a lot of free space between the molecules in a gas.
   c. There is a lot of free molecules in a space gas.
   d. There is the molecules in a gas, and then there is a lot of free space between.

4. Choose the correct way to write the underlined part of sentence 3.

   However, <u>gases and liquids</u> are very different from each other.

   f. Gases and Liquids
   g. gases and Liquids
   h. Gases and liquids
   j. No change is needed.

5. Choose the **best** way to combine the ideas in sentences 7 and 8 into one sentence.

> **The <u>molecules moves</u> very quickly. They often bump into each other.**

    a. The molecules move very quickly, and they often bump into each other.
    b. The molecules move very quickly often bump into each other.
    c. The molecules move, often bumps into each other very quickly.
    d. The molecules often move very quickly bump into each other.

6. Choose the correct way to write the underlined part of sentence 9.

> **If the gas gets hot or if it gets <u>squeazed</u> into a smaller space, the molecules hit each other more often.**

    f. squaeezed
    g. scueezed
    h. squeezed
    j. No change is needed.

7. Read sentence 12. It is poorly written.

> **They touch each other, but they are not attached even though they touch each other.**

Choose the **best** way to rewrite it so that it does not repeat ideas.

    a. They touch each other they are not attached even though they touch each other.
    b. They touch each other, but they are not attached and they touch each other.
    c. Even though they touch each other, they are not attached.
    d. Even though they touch each other, they are not attached but they touch each other.

8. Choose the correct way to write the underlined part of sentence 14.

   Liquids change to fit the shape of <u>its containers.</u>

   f. our containers.
   g. their containers.
   h. your containers.
   j. No change is needed.

9. Barbara wants to add this sentence to the paragraph that begins with sentence 11.

   For example, if you pour orange juice from the carton into your glass, it goes from being carton-shaped to being glass-shaped.

   Where would the sentence **best** fit?

   a. right after sentence 11
   b. right after sentence 12
   c. right after sentence 14
   d. right after sentence 16

10. Choose the correct way to write the underlined part of sentence 16.

    This is because <u>the molecules were already</u> close together.

    f. the molecules are already
    g. the molecules have been already
    h. the molecules will be already
    j. No change is needed.

11. Which one of these is **not** a complete sentence?

    a. The gas expands to fill a space.
    b. They often bump into each other.
    c. They can move freely and slide past each other.
    d. Impossible to squeeze a liquid into a smaller space.

Ian's fourth-grade class is learning about the Everglades, an area in Florida. His teacher asked each student to choose one living thing that grows in the Everglades and to describe it. Ian chose to write about mangroves. He wrote his rough draft, and now he needs your help editing and revising it.

Here is Ian's rough draft. Read it and then answer questions 1–10.

(1) There are many mangroves growing along the coast of Florida, these trees can live in salt water and fresh water, they like to live in estuaries. (2) An "estuary" is a place where fresh water meets salt water. (3) Like where a river meets the ocean.

(4) They're are not many plants that can live in salt water. (5) Salt can kill plants. (6) Mangroves have special ways of living in salt. (7) Black Mangrove trees have roots that stick out. (8) They can suck oxigen from the air. (9) Red mangroves grow right in the ocean, red mangroves have long roots that hold the trees up out of the water. (10) The trees look like they are up on stilts. (11) Its seeds start to sprout right on the tree.

(12) The roots of the mangrove tree makes a nice place for animals to live. (13) The leaves don't all fall off at once every fall. (14) They fall off a few at a time all year long. (15) Bacteria, fungi, worms, and crustaceans have plenty of good food.

1. Read sentence 1. It is poorly written.

    There are many mangroves growing along the coast of Florida, these trees can live in salt water and fresh water, they like to live in estuaries.

    Choose the **best** way to rewrite the sentence.

    a. There are many mangroves growing along the coast of Florida. These trees can live in salt water and fresh water, and they like to live in estuaries.
    b. There are many mangroves growing along the coast of Florida. In salt water and fresh water, and in estuaries.
    c. There are many mangroves growing along Florida, and salt water, and fresh water, and estuaries.
    d. There are many mangroves growing. Along the coast of Florida, these trees can live in salt water. And fresh water. They like to live in estuaries.

2. Choose the correct way to write the underlined part of sentence 4.

    <u>They're are not many plants</u> that can live in salt water.

    f. There are not many plants
    g. Their are not many plants
    h. They are not many plants
    j. No change is needed.

3. Which one of these is **not** a complete sentence?

    a. An "estuary" is a place where fresh water meets salt water.
    b. Like where a river meets the ocean.
    c. Salt can kill plants.
    d. They fall off a few at a time all year long.

4. Choose the correct way to write the underlined part of sentence 7.

    <u>Black Mangrove trees</u> have roots that stick out.

    f. black mangrove trees
    g. Black Mangrove Trees
    h. Black mangrove trees
    j. No change is needed.

5. Ian wants to change sentence 7 so that it is more specific.

    Black Mangrove trees have roots that <u>stick out.</u>

    Choose the **best** way to rewrite the underlined part of the sentence.

    a. poke out.
    b. point all the way down into the water.
    c. go out of the water.
    d. grow out of the water like straws.

6. Choose the correct way to write the underlined part of sentence 12.

   <u>The roots of the mangrove tree makes</u> a nice place for animals to live.

   f. The roots of the mangrove trees making
   g. The roots of the mangrove tree make
   h. The roots of the mangrove tree made
   j. No change is needed.

7. Read sentence 9. It is poorly written.

   Red mangroves grow right in the ocean, red mangroves have long roots that hold the trees up out of the water.

   Choose the **best** way to rewrite the sentence so that it does not repeat ideas.
   a. Red mangroves grow right in the ocean, red mangroves having long roots holding the trees up out of the water.
   b. Red mangroves grow right in the ocean, red mangroves have long roots. They hold the trees up out of the water.
   c. Red mangroves grow right in the ocean, and their long roots hold the trees up out of the water.
   d. Red mangroves grow right in the ocean, red mangroves, and they have long roots, and they hold the trees up out of the water.

8. Choose the correct way to write the underlined part of sentence 15.

   <u>Bacteria, fungi, worms, and crustaceans</u> have plenty of good food.

   f. Bacteria, fungi, worms, and, crustaceans
   g. Bacteria, fungi, worms and crustaceans
   h. Bacteria fungi worms and, crustaceans
   j. No change is needed.

9. Ian wants to add this sentence to the paragraph that begins with sentence 4.

   The seeds are coated with wax for protection.

   Where would the sentence **best** fit?

   a. right after sentence 4
   b. right after sentence 6
   c. right after sentence 9
   d. right after sentence 11

10. Choose the correct way to write the underlined part of sentence 8.

   They can suck <u>oxigen</u> from the air.

   f. oxygen
   g. O2
   h. oxagen
   j. No change is needed.

Anna is in the fourth grade. Her class is studying the lives of artists. Her teacher asked each student to choose one artist and to write a biography. Anna chose to write about Vincent van Gogh. She took notes at the library, organized them, and wrote her rough draft. Now she needs your help editing and revising it.

Here is Anna's rough draft. Read it and then answer questions 1–11.

(1) Vincent van Gogh was a Dutch painter, Vincent van Gogh was born in 1853. (2) His <u>Father</u> was a <u>Pastor</u>. (3) His parents had six children.

(4) <u>Vincent's parent's didn't want him to be</u> an artist. (5) They wanted him to be an art salesman like his Uncle Cent. (6) He went <u>to London.</u> (7) In London, he saw many poor people. (8) He gave up selling art he started to help poor people. (9) He became a preacher but, after a while, he lost his job.

(10) Vincent finally decided to become an artist in 1880. (11) <u>A rich painter helped paid for him</u> to go to art school.

(12) People didn't like his painting at first. (13) He painted a picture called "The Potato Eaters." (14) It was not a very pretty-looking picture. (15) Showing a poor farm family eating dinner.

(16) Vincent painted many other pictures. (17) He painted landscapes and <u>portrits</u>, too. (18) Bright colors and strong brushstrokes, he became known for.

(19) I can't believe that Vincent van Gogh only sold one painting, "The Red Vineyard," in his whole life. (20) After he died in 1890, his other works became famous.

1. Read sentence 1. It is poorly written.

   Vincent van Gogh was a Dutch painter, Vincent van Gogh was born in 1853.

   Which one of these is the **best** way to rewrite it?

   a. Vincent van Gogh was a Dutch painter, Vincent van Gogh being born in 1853.
   b. Vincent van Gogh, a Dutch painter, Vincent van Gogh was born in 1853.
   c. Vincent van Gogh was born in 1853, and Vincent van Gogh was a Dutch painter.
   d. Vincent van Gogh, a Dutch painter, was born in 1853.

2. Choose the correct way to write the underlined part of sentence 2.

    His <u>Father was a Pastor</u>.

    f. father was a Pastor.
    g. Father was a pastor.
    h. father was a pastor.
    j. No change is needed.

3. Anna wants to add this sentence to the paragraph that begins with sentence 1.

    Vincent's brother, Theo, was his close friend.

    Where would the sentence **best** fit?

    a. right after sentence 3
    b. right after sentence 2
    c. right after sentence 1
    d. right before sentence 1

4. Choose the correct way to write the underlined part of sentence 6.

    He went <u>to London</u>.

    f. too London.
    g. two London.
    h. into London.
    j. No change is needed.

5. Choose the **best** way to combine the ideas in sentences 6 and 7 into one sentence.

    He went <u>to London</u>. In London, he saw many poor people.

    a. He went to London, in London, he saw many poor people.
    b. He went to London and in London, he saw many poor people.
    c. He went to London, where he saw many poor people.
    d. He went to London, where in London, he saw many poor people.

6. Choose the correct way to write the underlined part of sentence 4.

    <u>Vincent's parent's didn't want him to be</u> an artist.

    f. Vincent's parents didn't want him to be
    g. Vincent's parents' didn't want him to be
    h. Vincent's parents's didn't want him to be
    j. No change is needed.

7. Read sentence 8. It is poorly written.

    He gave up selling art he started to help poor people.

    Choose the **best** way to rewrite the sentence.

    a. He gave up. Selling art to help poor people.
    b. He gave up selling art and helping poor people.
    c. He gave up selling art started to help poor people.
    d. He gave up selling art, and he started to help poor people.

8. Choose the correct way to write the underlined part of sentence 17.

    He painted landscapes and <u>portrits</u>, too.

    f. portrats
    g. portraits
    h. portrates
    j. No change is needed.

9. Which one of these is **not** a complete sentence?

    a. They wanted him to be an art salesman like his Uncle Cent.
    b. He became a preacher but, after a while, he lost his job.
    c. Showing a poor farm family eating dinner.
    d. After he died in 1890, his other work became famous.

10. Choose the correct way to write the underlined part of sentence 11.

<u>A rich painter helped paid for him</u> to go to art school.

    f.   A rich painter helped paying for him
    g.   A rich painter helped will pay for him
    h.   A rich painter helped pay for him
    j.   No change is needed.

11. Read sentence 18. It is poorly written.

Bright colors and strong brushstrokes, he became known for.

Choose the **best** way to rewrite this sentence.

    a.   He became known for bright colors and strong brushstrokes.
    b.   He became knowing bright colors and strong brushstrokes.
    c.   Bright colors and strong brushstrokes became known for him.
    d.   He knew bright colors and strong brushstrokes.

123

Travis is in the fourth grade. His class is studying global warming. His teacher has asked each student to find out what he or she could do to reduce global warming. Travis brainstormed his ideas, wrote them in a graphic organizer, and wrote his rough draft. Now he needs your help editing and revising it.

Here is Travis's rough draft. Read it and then answer questions 1–10.

(1) The world is getting <u>warmer and warmer</u>. (2) <u>Its happening</u> so slowly that we can't feel it. (3) The average temperature has only gone up a little in the past one hundred years. (4) Some scientists are worried about global warming. (5) They think it will cause floods and bad weather someday. (6) They think it will hurt many plants and animals.

(7) There are gases in the air called "greenhouse gases." (8) They act like a greenhouse they trap the sun's heat, they make the earth warmer. (9) My father built a sundial in our backyard. (10) <u>Power plants makes</u> greenhouse gases.

(11) <u>There were some things</u> you can do to reduce greenhouse gases. (12) You can use less electricity you can recycle your cans and bottles. (13) You can save energy by walking or riding a bike instead of taking a car. (14) You can plant a tree. (15) Trees use up carbon dioxide, and that's good because carbon dioxide is an important greenhouse gas. (16) You can make a <u>diffrence!</u>

1. Travis wants to change sentence 3 so that it is more specific.

   The average temperature has only gone up <u>a little</u> in the past one hundred years.

   Choose the **best** way to rewrite the underlined part of the sentence.

   a. just a tiny bit
   b. only one degree
   c. a small amount
   d. very little

2. Choose the correct way to write the underlined part of sentence 1.

The world is getting <u>warmer and warmer.</u>

    f. warmer, and warmer.
    g. warmer, and, warmer.
    h. warmer, warmer.
    j. No change is needed.

3. Read sentence 8. It is poorly written.

They act like a greenhouse they trap the sun's heat, they make the earth warmer.

Choose the **best** way to rewrite the sentence.

    a. They act like a greenhouse trap the sun's heat. They make the earth warmer.
    b. They act like a greenhouse trap. The sun's heat, they make the earth warmer.
    c. Acting like a greenhouse trapping the sun's heat, making the earth warmer.
    d. They act like a greenhouse. They trap the sun's heat, and they make the earth warmer.

4. Choose the correct way to write the underlined part of sentence 2.

<u>Its happening</u> so slowly that we can't feel it.

    f. It's happening
    g. Its' happening
    h. It happening
    j. No change is needed.

5. Choose the sentence that does **not** belong in the paragraph that begins with sentence 7.

   a. sentence 7
   b. sentence 10
   c. sentence 9
   d. sentence 8

6. Choose the correct way to write the underlined part of sentence 10.

   <u>Power plants makes</u> greenhouse gases.

   f. Powers plants makes
   g. Power plants make
   h. Power plant make
   j. No change is needed.

7. Read sentence 12. It is poorly written.

   You can use less electricity you can recycle your cans and bottles.

   Choose the **best** way to rewrite the sentence.

   a. You can use less electricity, and you can recycle your cans and bottles.
   b. You can use less electricity with your cans and bottles.
   c. You can use less electricity. Can recycle your cans and bottles.
   d. Less electricity. Recycle your cans and bottles, you can.

8. Choose the correct way to write the underlined part of sentence 16.

You can make a <u>diffrence!</u>

   f.   differrence!
   g. diference!
   h. difference!
   j.   No change is needed.

9. Choose the sentence that **best** fits right after sentence 13.

   a. The earth turns so that each spot gets sunlight for part of the day.
   b. Termites have creatures in their guts that help them to digest wood.
   c. Volcanoes can affect global temperatures.
   d. You can put solar panels on your house.

10. Choose the correct way to write the underlined part of sentence 11.

<u>There were some things</u> you can do to reduce greenhouse gases.

   f.   There are some things
   g. There will be some things
   h. There be some things
   j.   No change is needed.

Edward's fourth-grade class is learning about transportation. His teacher asked each student to describe the history of one form of transportation. Edward chose to describe the bicycle. He took notes and wrote his rough draft, and now he needs your help editing and revising it.

Here is Edward's rough draft. Read it and then answer questions 1—11.

(1) The first bicycle ever made was not even called a "bicycle," the first bicycle ever made was called a "walking machine." (2) It was just a bar with two wheels and a handle didn't even have pedals. (3) <u>People have to push</u> with their feet on the ground. (4) They used the walking machine to glide around the park or garden. (5) I got a new bicycle for my birthday.

(6) In 1865, <u>The Velocipede</u> was invented. (7) The name, "velocipede," means "fast foot." (8) <u>People</u> also called it the "bone shaker." (9) It had a huge front wheel. (10) It was made of heavy wood and metal. (11) It did have pedals. (12) When a rider went down a cobblestone street. (13) He got a really bumpy ride! (14) If he hit a bump, he fell over the big wheel onto his head!

(15) In 1870, the first machines called bicycles were invented. (16) Bicycles <u>kept getting more better and more better</u>. (17) <u>It became</u> safe and comfortable. (18) In the 1890s, everyone wanted a bicycle. (19) Bicycle riders formed a club called the League of American Wheelman. (20) Today it is called the League of American Bicyclists.

1. Edward wants to add this sentence to the paragraph that begins with sentence 1.

   Baron von Drais invented the walking machine in 1817.

   Where would the sentence **best** fit?

   a. right after sentence 1
   b. right after sentence 4
   c. right after sentence 5
   d. right after sentence 2

2. Choose the correct way to write the underlined part of sentence 3.

   <u>People have to push</u> with their feet on the ground.

   f. People were having to push
   g. People had to push
   h. People will have to push
   j. No change is needed.

3. Read sentence 1. It is poorly written.

   The first bicycle ever made was not even called a "bicycle," the first bicycle ever made was called a "walking machine."

   Choose the **best** way to rewrite the sentence so that it does not repeat ideas.

   a. The first bicycle ever made was not even called a "bicycle," the first bicycle ever made. It was called a "walking machine."
   b. The first bicycle ever made was not even called a "bicycle." It was called a "walking machine."
   c. The first bicycle ever made was not even called a "bicycle," and the first bicycle ever made was called a "walking machine."
   d. The first bicycle ever made. It was not even called a "bicycle." The first bicycle ever made a "walking machine."

4. Choose the correct way to write the underlined part of sentence 17.

   <u>It became</u> safe and comfortable.

   f. We became
   g. She became
   h. They became
   j. No change is needed.

5. Read sentence 2. It is poorly written.

   It was just a bar with two wheels and a handle didn't even have pedals.

   Choose the **best** way to rewrite the sentence.

   a. It was just a bar with two wheels and a handle it didn't even have pedals.
   b. It was just a bar it had two wheels and a handle it didn't even have pedals.
   c. It was just a bar, and it had two wheels, and a handle, and it didn't even have pedals.
   d. It was just a bar with two wheels and a handle. It didn't even have pedals.

6. Choose the correct way to write the underlined part of sentence 6.

   In 1865, <u>The Velocipede</u> was invented.

   f. the velocipede
   g. The velocipede
   h. the Velocipede
   j. No change is needed.

7. Choose the sentence that does **not** belong in the paragraph that begins with sentence 1.

   a. sentence 1
   b. sentence 5
   c. sentence 3
   d. sentence 2

130

8. Choose the correct way to write the underlined part of sentence 8.

   People also called it the "bone shaker."

   f. Peeple
   g. Peopel
   h. Peepul
   j. No change is needed.

9. Choose the **best** way to combine the ideas in sentences 9 and 10 into one sentence.

   It had a huge front wheel. It was made of heavy wood and metal.

   a. It had a huge front wheel it was made of heavy wood and metal.
   b. It had a huge, heavy front wheel, and wood and metal.
   c. It had a huge front wheel, and it was made of heavy wood and metal.
   d. It had a huge front, a wheel it was made of, and heavy wood and metal.

10. Choose the correct way to write the underlined part of sentence 16.

    Bicycles kept getting more better and more better.

    f. kept getting better and better.
    g. kept getting better and best.
    h. kept getting the best of all.
    j. No change is needed.

11. Which one of these is **not** a complete sentence?

    a. It was made of heavy wood and metal.
    b. He got a really bumpy ride!
    c. If he hit a bump, he fell over the big wheel onto his head!
    d. When a rider went down a cobblestone street.

131

Natalie is in the fourth grade. Her class is learning about agriculture. Her teacher asked each student to research one type of crop and to describe how it gets from the farm to the kitchen table. Natalie chose to write about soybeans. She took notes from an encyclopedia, organized them, and wrote her rough draft. Now she needs your help editing and revising it.

Here is Natalie's rough draft. Read it and then answer questions 1–10.

(1) <u>People has been</u> growing soybeans for thousands of years. (2) Soybeans are very high in protein. (3) The United States grows more soybeans than any other country. (4) Our soybean crops cover a lot of land!

(5) Soybeans are grown this way. (6) Farmers plant soybean plants <u>in may or june</u>. (7) In six to eight weeks, <u>white or purple flowers bloom</u>. (8) Then the pods grow. (9) Each pod has two or three soybeans inside. (10) The soybeans are also called "seeds." (11) In the late summer or early fall, farmers harvest the seeds. (12) They use machines called "combines." (13) These machines cut the plants. (14) They clean the seeds at the same time. (15) The farmers sell the seeds.

(16) Soybeans are used to make many different things. (17) Machines crush the beans and pressing them from oil. (18) Most of the soybeans are used to make food for farm animals. (19) Some are used to make <u>vegtable</u> oil for cooking. (20) Some are used to make soy grits or soy flour. (21) Maybe <u>the cereal that your had for breakfast</u> this morning had soy in it.

1. Natalie wants to change sentence 4 so that it is more specific.

    Our soybean crops cover <u>a lot of land!</u>

    Choose the **best** way to rewrite the underlined part of the sentence.

    a. a huge amount of land!
    b. many acres of land!
    c. more than sixty million acres of land!
    d. so much land, I can't believe it!

2. Choose the correct way to write the underlined part of sentence 1.

   People has been growing soybeans for thousands of years.

   f. People will have been
   g. People have been
   h. People had been
   j. No change is needed.

3. Choose the topic sentence for the paragraph that begins with sentence 5.

   a. Soybeans are grown this way.
   b. The soybeans are also called "seeds."
   c. They use machines called "combines."
   d. The farmers sell the seeds.

4. Choose the correct way to write the underlined part of sentence 6.

   Farmers plant soybean plants in may or june.

   f. in May or june.
   g. in may or June.
   h. in May or June.
   j. No change is needed.

5. Choose the **best** way to combine the ideas in sentences 13 and 14 into one sentence.

   These machines cut the plants. They clean the seeds at the same time.

   a. These machines cutting the plants, cleaning the seeds at the same time.
   b. These machines cut the plants and seeds at the same time.
   c. These machines they cut the plants they clean the seeds at the same time.
   d. These machines cut the plants and clean the seeds at the same time.

133

6. Choose the correct way to write the underlined part of sentence 19.

   Some are used to make <u>vegtable</u> oil for cooking.

   f. vegetable
   g. veggetable
   h. vegatable
   j. No change is needed.

7. Read sentence 17. It is poorly written.

   Machines crush the beans and pressing them from oil.

   Choose the **best** way to rewrite this sentence.

   a. Machines crushing the beans and pressing them from oil.
   b. Machines crush the beans. And pressing oil from them.
   c. Machines crush the beans and press oil from them.
   d. Machines crush the beans from pressing them.

8. Choose the correct way to write the underlined part of sentence 21.

   Maybe <u>the cereal that your had for breakfast</u> this morning had soy in it.

   f. the cereal that yours had for breakfast
   g. the cereal that you had for breakfast
   h. the cereal that yous had for breakfast
   j. No change is needed.

9. Choose the sentence that **best** fits right after sentence 19.

    a. The soybean belongs to the pea family.
    b. The soybean plant lives for only one year.
    c. The ancient Chinese considered soybeans to be their most important crop.
    d. Some soybeans are used to make "tofu."

10. Choose the correct way to write the underlined part of sentence 7.

    In six to eight weeks, <u>white or purple flowers bloom.</u>

    f. white or purple flowers blooms.
    g. white or purple flowers blooming.
    h. white or purple flowers bloomed.
    j. No change is needed.

Nasif is in the fourth grade. His class is studying geography. His teacher asked the students in the class to describe the plant life in the tundra. Nasif wrote his rough draft, and now he needs your help editing and revising it.

Here is Nasif's rough draft. Read it and then answer questions 1–11.

(1) The <u>arctic</u> tundra is a very cold place at the top of the world. (2) There are no trees it is very windy and dry. (3) Some parts are hilly, and some parts are flat. (4) The climate is very harsh for growing things.

(5) <u>The tundra have</u> very short summers. (6) The ground thaws only a few inches deep. (7) Under that, <u>there are still ice.</u> (8) The plants only have very short roots the plants they don't grow to be very tall. (9) Neither did my mother's African violet.

(10) There are a few things that grow in the tundra. (11) Grass and wildflowers cover the ground in the summertime. (12) <u>There leaves are very small</u> because small leaves can live in the cold better than large leaves. (13) Some of the plants are covered with tiny hairs. (14) Helps to protect them more.

(15) Tundra plants bloom and make seeds very quickly. (16) They only have <u>an short time.</u> (17) When winter comes, the roots and seeds will be the only things that survive.

1. Read sentence 2. It is poorly written.

    There are no trees it is very windy and dry.

    Choose the **best** way to rewrite the sentence.

    a. There are no trees, very windy and dry.
    b. There are no trees being very windy and dry.
    c. There are no trees, and very windy and dry.
    d. There are no trees, and it is very windy and dry.

2. Choose the correct way to write the underlined part of sentence 5.

   <u>The tundra have</u> very short summers.

   f. The tundra has
   g. The tundra having
   h. The tundra had
   j. No change is needed.

3. Read sentence 8. It is poorly written.

   The plants only have very short roots the plants they don't grow to be very tall.

   Choose the **best** way to rewrite the sentence so that it does not repeat ideas.

   a. The plants only have very short roots so that the plants they don't grow to be very tall.
   b. The plants only have very short roots, so they don't grow to be very tall.
   c. The plants only have very short roots the plants not growing very tall.
   d. The plants only have very short roots and the plants don't grow to be very tall.

4. Choose the correct way to write the underlined part of sentence 1.

   The <u>arctic</u> tundra is a very cold place at the top of the world.

   f. arrtic
   g. artctic
   h. artic
   j. No change is needed.

5. Choose the sentence that does **not** belong in the paragraph that begins with sentence 5.

    a. sentence 7
    b. sentence 9
    c. sentence 6
    d. sentence 8

6. Choose the correct way to write the underlined part of sentence 16.

    They only have <u>an short time.</u>

    f. the short time.
    g. any short time.
    h. a short time.
    j. No change is needed.

7. Choose the topic sentence for the paragraph that begins with sentence 10.

    a. There are a few things that grow in the tundra.
    b. Grass and wildflowers cover the ground in the summertime.
    c. Some of the plants are covered with tiny hairs.
    d. Tundra plants bloom and make seeds very quickly.

8. Choose the correct way to write the underlined part of sentence 12.

    <u>There leaves are very small</u> because small leaves can live in the cold better than large leaves.

    f. They're leaves are very small
    g. Theyre leaves are very small
    h. Their leaves are very small
    j. No change is needed.

9. Choose the sentence that **best** fits right after sentence 10.

    a. The ground is lumpy and cracked.
    b. Winter days are short.
    c. Moss grows near streams in the tundra.
    d. The tundra is close to the North Pole.

10. Choose the correct way to write the underlined part of sentence 7.

    Under that, <u>there are still ice.</u>

    f. there is still ice.
    g. there will be still ice.
    h. there being still ice.
    j. No change is needed.

11. Which one of these is **not** a complete sentence?

    a. Some parts are hilly, and some parts are flat.
    b. The ground thaws only a few inches deep.
    c. Some of the plants are covered with tiny hairs.
    d. Helps to protect them more.

Marcus is in the fourth grade. His class is studying geography. His teacher asked each student to write about how living on a mountain affects people. Marcus took notes from his library book, organized them, and wrote his rough draft. Now he needs your help editing and revising it.

Here is Marcus's rough draft. Read it and then answer questions 1–10.

(1) Living on a mountain is different from living at sea level. (2) People living in small villages. (3) <u>Mountain peaks separates</u> the villages. (4) So the people don't know the people in the other villages. (5) They don't communicate with each other very much. (6) This is true in Switzerland, where there is a very large mountain range called the "Alps." (7) Swiss chocolate is delicious. (8) In Switzerland's Alps, people speak four different languages. (9) They speak those languages in so many different ways.

(10) People who live on mountains sometimes have problems. (11) If they live high on the mountain, they probably have cold weather and rough land if they live high on the mountain. (12) If the mountain is beautiful, visitors might want to take a vacation there. (13) Tourists like to go <u>skiing camping and hiking.</u> (14) However, if there are <u>to many tourists,</u> it can cause trouble. (15) Tourists bring more pollution. (16) Builders of hotels and restaurants cut down trees in the <u>forrest.</u> (17) This can cause erosion, landslides, avalanches, or floods.

1. Which one of these is **not** a complete sentence?

    a. People living in small villages.
    b. They don't communicate with each other very much.
    c. If the mountain is beautiful, visitors might want to take a vacation there.
    d. Tourists bring more pollution.

2. Choose the sentence that does **not** belong in the paragraph that begins with sentence 1.

    f. sentence 7
    g. sentence 9
    h. sentence 10
    j. sentence 2

3. Choose the correct way to write the underlined part of sentence 3.

Mountain peaks separates the villages.

a. Mountain peaks separate
b. Mountain peak separates
c. Mountain peaks separating
d. No change is needed.

4. Choose the correct way to write the underlined part of sentence 16.

Builders of hotels and restaurants cut down trees in the forrest.

f. foresst.
g. forest.
h. forrist.
j. No change is needed.

5. Choose the correct way to write the underlined part of sentence 13.

Tourists like to go skiing camping and hiking.

a. skiing and camping and hiking.
b. skiing, camping, and, hiking.
c. skiing, camping, and hiking.
d. No change is needed.

6. Choose the correct way to write the underlined part of sentence 14.

However, if there are to many tourists, it can cause trouble.

f. too many tourists
g. two many tourists
h. 2 many tourists
j. No change is needed.

7. Read sentence 11. It is poorly written.

   If they live high on the mountain, they probably have cold weather and rough land if they live high on the mountain.

   Choose the **best** way to rewrite the sentence so that it does not repeat ideas.

   a.   If they live high on the mountain that probably has cold weather and rough land.

   b.   If they live high on the mountain, they probably have cold weather, and rough land if they live high on the mountain.

   c.   If they live high on the mountain, they probably have cold weather, and they probably have rough land, too, if they live high on the mountain.

   d.   If they live high on the mountain, they probably have cold weather and rough land.

8. Marcus wants to change sentence 9 so that it is more specific.

   They speak those languages <u>in so many different ways.</u>

   Choose the **best** way to rewrite the underlined part of the sentence.

   f.   a large number of ways.

   g.   in very many ways.

   h.   in hundreds of ways.

   j.   in a huge amount of ways.

9. Marcus wants to add this sentence to the paragraph that begins with sentence 10.

Tourists spend money on the mountain, and that is good for the mountain people.

Where would the sentence **best** fit?

a. right after sentence 15
b. right after sentence 10
c. right after sentence 13
d. right after sentence 17

10. Choose the **best** way to combine the ideas in sentences 3 and 4 into one sentence.

<u>Mountain peaks separates</u> the villages. So the people don't know the people in the other villages.

f. Mountain peaks separate the villages, the people don't know the people in the other villages.
g. Mountain peaks separate the villages, so the people don't know the people in the other villages.
h. Mountain peaks separate the villages who don't know the people in the other villages.
j. Mountain peaks separate the villages not knowing the people in the other villages.

Luis's fourth-grade health class is studying nutrition. His teacher asked each student to choose one vitamin and to describe how it works in the body. Luis chose to write about vitamin A. He did his research in the school library. He took notes and organized them. Then he wrote his rough draft. Now he needs your help editing and revising it.

Here is Luis's rough draft. Read it and then answer questions 1–10.

(1) Vitamin A is a very important vitamin. (2) It is also called "retinol." (3) Vitamin A is only found in animals. (4) We can get it from eggs, liver, and milk. (5) What if we don't like eggs, liver, or milk? (6) Then we can make our own <u>Vitamin A</u> from carotenes. (7) Vitamin C is a water-soluble vitamin.

(8) Vitamin A does a lot of good things for the body. (9) It <u>helps babys bones</u> and teeth grow. (10) <u>They keep</u> skin healthy. (11) It helps to make white blood cells. (12) You might get sick from an infection that doesn't have enough of them.

(13) Vitamin A helps you to see <u>when their is</u> very little light. (14) When people don't have enough vitamin A, they can get night blindness when they don't have enough. (15) It is one of the first signs that someone needs more vitamin A. (16) In <u>ancient</u> Egypt they knew about this. (17) They gave the people liver. (18) Their night blindness went away.

1. Choose the sentence that does **not** belong in the paragraph that begins with sentence 1.

   a. sentence 5
   b. sentence 2
   c. sentence 7
   d. sentence 6

2. Choose the correct way to write the underlined part of sentence 9.

   It <u>helps babys bones</u> and teeth grow.

   f. helps baby's bones
   g. helps babies' bones
   h. helps babys' bones
   j. No change is needed.

3. Luis wants to add this sentence to the paragraph that begins with sentence 1.

    There are carotenes in cantaloupes, carrots, sweet potatoes, and dark green leafy vegetables.

    Where would the sentence **best** fit?

    a. right after sentence 1
    b. right after sentence 6
    c. right after sentence 2
    d. right after sentence 3

4. Choose the correct way to write the underlined part of sentence 10.

    <u>They keep</u> skin healthy.

    f. He keeps
    g. We keep
    h. It keeps
    j. No change is needed.

5. Read sentence 12. It is poorly written.

    You might get sick from an infection that doesn't have enough of them.

    Choose the **best** way to rewrite this sentence.

    a. You might get sick from an infection if you don't have enough of them.
    b. You might get sick if an infection has enough of them.
    c. You might get sick with enough of them from an infection.
    d. You might get sick from an infection. That doesn't have enough of them.

6. Choose the correct way to write the underlined part of sentence 13.

   Vitamin A helps you to see <u>when their is</u> very little light.

   f. when there is
   g. when theres is
   h. when they're is
   j. No change is needed.

7. Read sentence 14. It is poorly written.

   When people don't have enough vitamin A, they can get night blindness when they don't have enough.

   Choose the **best** way to rewrite the sentence so that it does not repeat ideas.

   a. When people don't have enough vitamin A. They can get night blindness when they don't have enough.
   b. When people don't have enough vitamin A, they can get night blindness. When they don't have enough.
   c. When people don't have enough vitamin A, they can get, if they don't have enough, night blindness.
   d. When people don't have enough vitamin A, they can get night   blindness.

8. Choose the correct way to write the underlined part of sentence 16.

   In <u>ancient</u> Egypt they knew about this.

   f. anchient
   g. anchant
   h. anchent
   j. No change is needed.

146

9. Choose the **best** way to combine the ideas in sentences 17 and 18 into one sentence.

   They gave the people liver. Their night blindness went away.

   a. They gave the people liver, and their night blindness went away.
   b. They gave the people whose night blindness went away liver.
   c. They gave the people liver with night blindness.
   d. They gave the people liver and night blindness that went away.

10. Choose the correct way to write the underlined part of sentence 6.

    Then we can make our own <u>Vitamin A</u> from carotenes.

    f. Vitamin a
    g. vitamin a
    h. vitamin A
    j. No change is needed.

Anna's health class is studying water safety. Her teacher asked each student to write a fictional story describing a water rescue. Anna wrote an outline, and then she wrote a rough draft. Now she needs your help editing and revising it.

Here is Anna's rough draft. Read it and then answer questions 1–10.

(1) <u>My friend, Katie, and, I, were fishing</u> at the stream by her house. (2) Suddenly, Katie tripped <u>on an rock.</u> (3) She fell right into the water. (4) The water was deeper than it looked. (5) She <u>couldnt</u> get out, and she started to panic. (6) She started to scream.

(7) Then I <u>remembered</u> the four steps to water rescue: reach, throw, row, and don't go. (8) The first thing I tried was reaching. (9) I found a tree root, and I held onto it sticking out of the ground. (10) I reached out to her <u>with me other hand.</u> (11) She tried to reach me our arms weren't long enough. (12) The water started to carry her down the stream. (13) I started yelling for help.

(14) The next thing I tried was throwing. (15) I got a rope from my backpack. (16) I tied it around a log. (17) I threw it out to her. (18) It was so heavy that I had to throw it again. (19) The second time, she grabbed it! (20) Then she was safe enough not to drown.

(21) I could not pull her in because I was not strong enough. (22) I could not row to her because I had no boat. (23) Fortunately, some other people heard me screaming. (24) Came and pulled Katie out of the water.

1. Read sentence 9. It is poorly written.

I found a tree root, and I held onto it sticking out of the ground.

Choose the **best** way to rewrite this sentence.

a. I found a tree root, and I held onto it, sticking out of the ground.
b. I found a tree root, sticking out of the ground, holding onto it.
c. I found a tree root sticking out of the ground, and I held onto it.
d. I found a tree root holding onto it sticking out of the ground.

2. Choose the correct way to write the underlined part of sentence 1.

   <u>My friend, Katie, and, I, were fishing</u> at the stream by her house.

   f. My friend, Katie, and I were fishing
   g. My friend, Katie and I were fishing
   h. My friend Katie, and I, were fishing
   j. No change is needed.

3. Read sentence 11. It is poorly written.

   She tried to reach me our arms weren't long enough.

   Choose the **best** way to rewrite the sentence.

   a. She tried to reach me our arms not being long enough.
   b. She tried to reach each other our arms weren't long enough.
   c. She tried to reach me with her arm. Weren't long enough.
   d. She tried to reach me, but our arms weren't long enough.

4. Choose the correct way to write the underlined part of sentence 5.

   She <u>couldnt</u> get out, and she started to panic.

   f. could'nt
   g. couldn't
   h. couldnt'
   j. No change is needed.

5. Choose the topic sentence for the paragraph that begins with sentence 14.

   a. The next thing I tried was throwing.
   b. I got a rope from my backpack.
   c. I threw it out to her.
   d. It was so heavy that I had to throw it again.

6. Choose the correct way to write the underlined part of sentence 10.

I reached out to her <u>with me other hand.</u>

   f.   with my other hand.
   g.   with I other hand.
   h.   with the other hand.
   j.   No change is needed.

7. Choose the **best** way to combine the ideas in sentences 16 and 17 into one sentence.

I tied it around a log. I threw it out to her.

   a.   I tied it around a log threw it out to her.
   b.   I tied it around a log that threw it out to her.
   c.   I tied it around a log and threw it out to her.
   d.   I tied and threw it around a log out to her.

8. Choose the correct way to write the underlined part of sentence 2.

Suddenly, Katie tripped <u>on an rock.</u>

   f.   on the rock.
   g.   on a rock.
   h.   on a/an rock.
   j.   No change is needed.

9. Which one of these is **not** a complete sentence?

   a.   She fell right into the water.
   b.   The first thing I tried was reaching.
   c.   The water started to carry her down the stream.
   d.   Came and pulled Katie out of the water.

10. Choose the correct way to write the underlined part of sentence 7.

> **Then I <u>remembered</u> the four steps to water rescue:
> reach, throw, row, and don't go.**

    f.   rememmbered

    g.   rememberred

    h.   remembbered

    j.   No change is needed.

Valerie's fourth-grade class is discussing ways to handle peer pressure. Her teacher asked the students to brainstorm their ideas in small groups. Then she asked each student to write a summary of his or her group's ideas. Valerie did her rough draft, and now she needs your help editing and revising it.

Here is Valerie's rough draft. Read it and then answer questions 1–10.

---

(1) <u>Here are</u> some ways to handle "peer pressure." (2) Peer pressure is when other kids try to get you to do something. (3) When they try to get you to do something wrong. (4) That's bad peer pressure! (5) Don't do it!

(6) It is very <u>importent</u> to have values. (7) Values are what you believe in. (8) For example, your values might tell you that <u>it wrong to lie</u>. (9) Your values might tell you that it's wrong to steal. (10) Pay attention to your own feelings instead of to your peers do what you feel is right.

(11) Make good friends who don't get you in trouble. (12) Hang out with kids who don't <u>cut class smoke or drink.</u> (13) Make friends who are honest, not liars. (14) Try to make friends who have the same values as you.

(15) Doing bad things try to stay away from kids who are. (16) If they try to get you to do something wrong, say that you don't want to do it. (17) Talk to your <u>parents or your Teacher</u> if they keep bothering you.

---

1. Which one of these is **not** a complete sentence?

   a. When they try to get you to do something wrong.
   b. Values are what you believe in.
   c. Make good friends who don't get you in trouble.
   d. Make friends who are honest, not liars.

2. Choose the correct way to write the underlined part of sentence 1.

   <u>Here are</u> some ways to handle "peer pressure."

   f. Hear are
   g. Here're
   h. Hear're
   j. No change is needed.

152

3. Choose the **best** way to combine the ideas in sentences 8 and 9 into one sentence.

> **For example, your values might tell you that it's wrong to lie. Your values might tell you that it's wrong to steal.**

   a. For example, your values might tell you that it's wrong to lie and your values might tell you that it's wrong to steal.
   b. For example, your values might tell you that it's wrong to lie, your values might tell you that it's wrong to steal.
   c. For example, your values might tell you that it's wrong to lie, might tell you that it's wrong to steal.
   d. For example, your values might tell you that it's wrong to lie or steal.

4. Read sentence 10. It is poorly written.

> **Pay attention to your own feelings instead of to your peers do what you feel is right.**

   Choose the **best** way to rewrite the sentence.

   f. Pay attention to your own feelings instead of doing what you feel is right.
   g. Pay attention to your own feelings instead. Of your peers do what you feel is right.
   h. Pay attention to your own feelings instead of to your peers, and do what you feel is right.
   j. Pay attention to your own feelings instead of to peers. Doing what you feel is right.

5. Choose the correct way to write the underlined part of sentence 6.

   It is very <u>importent</u> to have values.

   a. importint
   b. importtant
   c. important
   d. No change is needed.

6. Choose the correct way to write the underlined part of sentence 8.

    For example, your values might tell you that <u>it wrong to lie</u>.

    f. it's wrong to lie
    g. its wrong to lie
    h. its' wrong to lie
    j. No change is needed.

7. Choose the correct way to write the underlined part of sentence 17.

    Talk to your <u>parents or your Teacher</u> if they keep bothering you.

    a. Parents or your Teacher
    b. parents or your teacher
    c. Parents or your teacher
    d. No change is needed.

8. Read sentence 15. It is poorly written.

    Doing bad things try to stay away from kids who are.

    Choose the **best** way to rewrite this sentence.

    f. Doing bad things, try to stay away from kids.
    g. Try to stay away from doing bad things, kids who are.
    h. Try to stay away from kids who are doing bad things.
    j. Doing bad things to stay away from kids who try.

154

9. Choose the correct way to write the underlined part of sentence 12.

Hang out with kids who don't <u>cut class smoke or drink.</u>

   a. cut class, smoke, or drink.
   b. cut class or, smoke or, drink.
   c. cut class, smoke, or drink.
   d. No change is needed.

10. Choose the sentence that **best** fits right after sentence 16.

   f. Smoking can make you sick.
   g. Your family will appreciate it if you help with the chores every day.
   h. It's important to go to school every day.
   j. If your friend tells you to steal something, you can say, "No."

NOTES

Made in the USA
Middletown, DE
30 May 2020